Aunt Phil's Trunk Volume One

Teacher Guide

Bringing Alaska's history alive!

By
Laurel Downing Bill

Special credit and much appreciation to Nicole Cruz for her diligent efforts to create the best student workbook and teacher guide available for Alaska history studies.

Aunt Phil's Trunk LLC, Anchorage, Alaska
www.auntphilstrunk.com

Copyright © 2017 by Laurel Downing Bill.

All rights reserved. No part of this book may be used or reproduced in any manner whatsoever without written permission from the author, except in the case of brief quotations embodied in critical articles and reviews.

International Standard Book Number 978-1-940479-27-9

Printed and bound in the United States of America.

First Printing 2017
First Printing Second Edition 2017
First Printing Third Edition 2018

Photo credits on the front cover, from top left: Native shaman with totem, Alaska State Library, Case and Draper Collection, ASL-P-39-782; Eskimo boy, Alaska State Library, Skinner Foundation, ASL-P44-11-002; Prospector, Alaska State Library, Skinner Foundation, ASL-P44-03-15; Athabascan woman, Anchorage Museum of History and Art, Crary-Henderson Collection, AMHA-b62-1-571; Gold miners, Alaska State Library, Harry T.Becker Collection, ASL-P67-052; Chilkoot Pass, Alaska State Library, Eric A. Hegg Collection, ASL-P124-04; Seal hunter, Alaska State Library, George A. Parks Collection, ASL-P240-210; Women mending boat, Alaska State Library, Rev. Samuel Spriggs Collection, ASL-P320-60; Teacher photo, Alaska State Library, J. Simpson MacKinnon Photo Collection, ASL-P14-073.

TABLE OF CONTENTS

Instructions *Aunt Phil's Trunk* Alaska History Curriculum	5
How to use this workbook at home	6
How to use this workbook for high school	7
How to use this workbook in the classroom	8
How to grade assignments	9
Rubric for Essay Questions	11
Rubric for Oral Presentations	12
Rubric for Enrichment Activities	12

UNIT 1: EARLY ALASKA

Lesson 1: Unanswered Questions	13
Lesson 2: Coping with the Unknown	15
Lesson 3: Explorers Ply Alaska Waters	18
Lesson 4: While the United States was Forming	22
Lesson 5: Island of Mystery	24
Lesson 6: Earthquakes Form Landscape	24
Review Lessons 1-6	26
Unit 1 Test	30

UNIT 2: LITTLE-KNOWN STORIES

Lesson 7: Natives Attack Russian Forts	32
Lesson 8: Woody Island's Icy Past	34
Lesson 9: Last Shot of the Civil War	36
Review Lessons 7-9	38
Unit 2 Test	44

UNIT 3: ALASKA BECOMES U.S. POSSESSION

Lesson 10: Seward's Folly Turns into Treasure	46
Lesson 11: Myth Surrounds Alaska Purchase	51
Lesson 12: Americans Flock North	47
Lesson 13: Apostle to the North	56
Lesson 14: Alaska's Mysterious Census-Taker	59
Review Lessons 10-14	62
Unit 3 Test	66

UNIT 4: ALASKA'S FIRST GOLD RUSH

Lesson 15: Gold Found in Southeast	68
Lesson 16: Exploring the Nile of Alaska	71
Lesson 17: Old John Bremner	76
Lesson 18: Rich Names Along the Koyukuk	78
Review Lessons 15-18	81
Unit 4 Test	84

TABLE OF CONTENTS

UNIT 5: DREAMS OF GOLD
Lesson 19: Alaska's Second Gold Rush 86
Lesson 20: Dreams of Salmon Turn to Gold 88
Lesson 21: Luckiest Man on the Klondike 91
Review Lessons 19-21 93
Unit 5 Test 96

UNIT 6: RUSH TO THE KLONDIKE
Lesson 22: Dawson is Born 100
Lesson 23: St. Michael Awakens 102
Lesson 24: Trails to Gold 106
Lesson 25: Gold Rush Trails Photo Essay 108
Lesson 26: Jack Dalton Builds Toll Road 110
Review Lessons 22-26 112
Unit 6 Test 116

UNIT 7: SEA CAPTAINS, SCOUNDRELS AND NUNS
Lesson 27: Sea Captain Stifles Mutiny 121
Lesson 28: Soapy Smith Heads to Skagway 123
Lesson 29: Miners Stampede to Nome 126
Lesson 30: Sisters of Providence Head to Nome 128

UNIT 8: NATIVES AND THE RUSH FOR GOLD
Lesson 31: Natives and the Rush for Gold 131
Lesson 32: Richest Native Woman in the North 134
Review Lessons 27-32 136
Unit 7-8 Test 140

Teacher notes 142-144

Welcome to *Aunt Phil's Trunk Volume One* Teacher Guide!

Have your student(s) read the chapters associated with each Unit. Then ask them to complete the lessons for that Unit to get a better understanding of Alaska's people and the events that helped shape Alaska's future.

I hope you and your student(s) enjoy your journey into Alaska's past from the arrival of the Native people up to around the year 1900.

Laurel Downing Bill, author

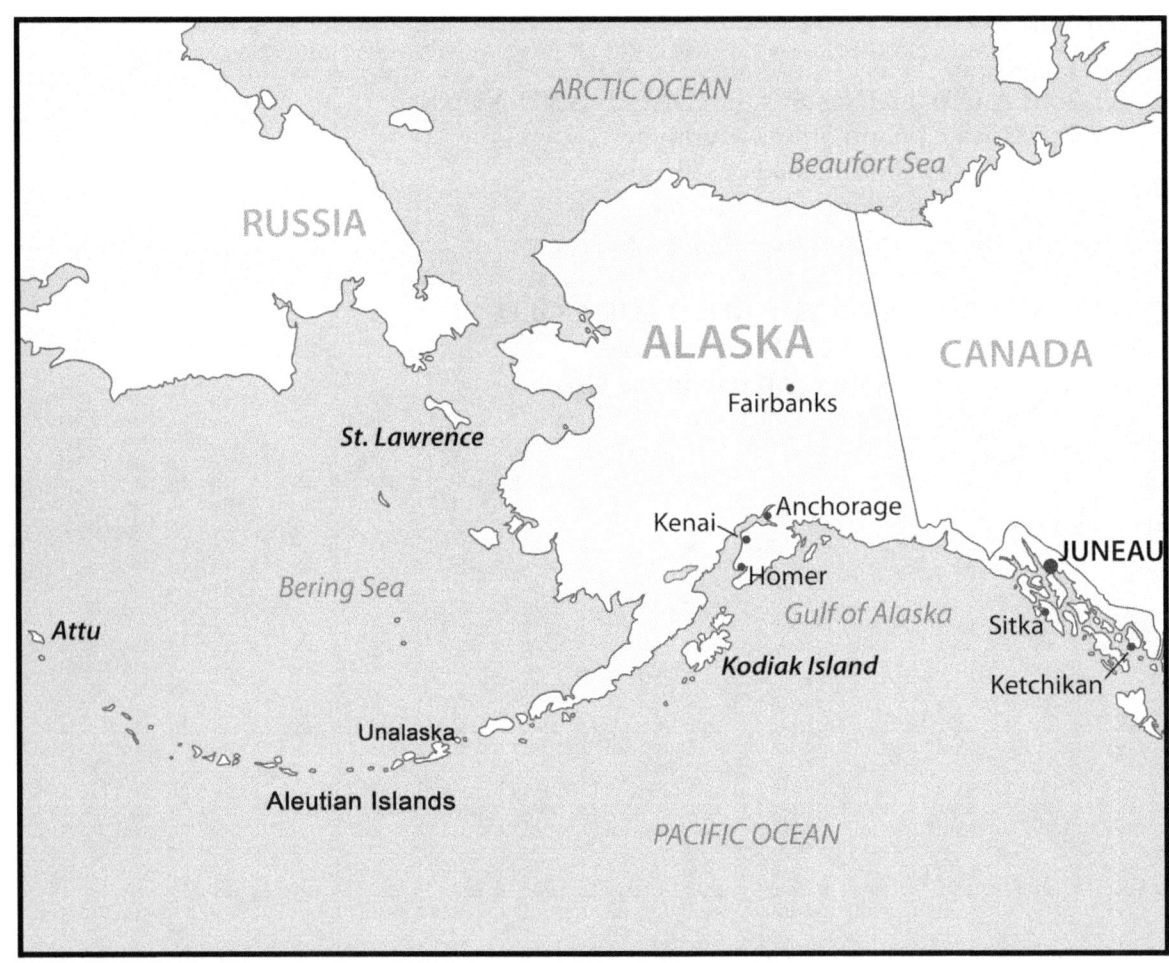

Instructions for using the *Aunt Phil's Trunk* Alaska History Curriculum

The *Aunt Phil's Trunk* Alaska History Curriculum is designed to be used in grades 4-8. High school students can use this curriculum, also, by taking advantage of the essay and enrichment activities throughout the book. The next few pages give further instruction on how to use this curriculum with middle school students, high school students and in classroom settings.

This curriculum can be taught in multiple grade levels by having your older students complete all reading, study guide work and enrichment activities independently. Students of all grade levels can participate in daily oral review by playing games like Jeopardy or Around the World.

This curriculum was developed so that students not only learn about Alaska's past, but they will have fun in the process. After every few lessons, they can test their knowledge through word scramble, word search and crossword puzzles.

Notes for parents with younger students:

1) Spiritual themes
The first chapters of this series contain detailed information about the spiritual beliefs of the Native people of Alaska. Alaska Native tribes are an important part of Alaska history and their spiritual beliefs greatly influenced their way of life. If you have concerns about introducing your child/children to spiritual topics that may vary greatly from your own family's beliefs, we encourage you to read over the chapters before your child so you can be ready to explain the belief system of early Native Alaskans, which in many cases was similar to those of indigenous people around the world.

2) Mature themes
Chapter 22 contains references to "good-time girls" during the gold rush. Parents of younger students may want to read through the chapter before your child/children and prepare yourself for any questions that may arise about these women.

How to use this workbook at home

Aunt Phil's Trunk Alaska History Curriculum is designed to be used in grades 4-8. High school students can use this curriculum, also, by taking advantage of the essay and enrichment activities throughout the book. The next page gives further instruction on how to use this curriculum with high school students.

This curriculum can be taught in multiple grade levels by having your older students complete all reading, study guide work and enrichment activities independently. Students of all grade levels can participate in daily oral review by playing games like Jeopardy or Around the World.

For Middle School Students:

1. **Facts to Know:** Read this section in the study guide with your student(s) before reading the chapter to get familiar with new terms that they will encounter in the reading.

2. **Read the chapter:** Read one chapter aloud to your student(s) or have them read it aloud to you. Older students may want to read independently.

3. **Comprehension Questions**: Younger students may answer the comprehension questions orally or write down their answers in the study guide. Use these questions to test your student(s) comprehension of the chapter. Older students should answer all questions in written form.

4. **Discussion Questions**: Have your student(s) answer these questions in a few sentences orally. Come up with follow-up questions to test your student(s) understanding of the material. Older students may answer discussion questions in written essay form.

5. **Map Work:** Some chapters will contain a map activity for your student(s) to learn more about the geography of the region that they are learning about.

6. **Enrichment and Online References:** (Optional) Assign enrichment activities as you see fit. Many of the online references are from the Alaska Humanities Forum website (http://www.akhistorycourse.org). We highly recommend this website for additional information, project ideas, etc.

7. **Unit Review:** At the end of a unit, your student will complete Unit Review questions and word puzzles in the study guide. Students should review all the chapters in the unit before completing the review. Parents may want to assist younger students with the word puzzles.

8. **Unit Test:** (Optional) There is an optional test that you can administer to your student(s) after they have completed all the unit work.

How to use this workbook for high school

1. **Facts to Know:** Your student(s) should read this section in the study guide before reading the chapter to get familiar with new terms that they will encounter.

2. **Read the chapter:** Your student(s) can read aloud or independently.

3. **Comprehension Questions:** Use these questions to test your student(s) comprehension of the chapter. Have your high schoolers write out their answers in complete sentences.

4. **Discussion Questions:** Have your student(s) answer these questions in a few sentences orally or write out their answer in essay form.

5. **Map Work:** Some chapters will contain a map activity for your student(s) to learn more about the geography of the region that they are learning about.

6. **Enrichment and Online References**: Once your high schooler has completed all the reading and study guide material for the chapter, assign additional reading from the enrichment material using the online links or book lists. Encourage your student(s) to explore topics of interest to them.

Many of the online references are from the Alaska Humanities Forum website. We highly recommend this website for additional information, project ideas, etc.

7. **Unit Review:** At the end of a unit, your student will complete Unit Review questions and word puzzles in their study guide. Students should review all the chapters in the unit before completing the review.

8. **Unit Test:** (Optional) There is an optional test that you can administer to your student(s) after they have completed all the unit work.

9. **Oral Presentation:** (Optional) Assign a 5-minute oral presentation on any topic in the reading. Encourage your student(s) to utilize the additional books and online resources to supplement the information in the textbook. Set aside a classroom day for your student(s) to share their presentations.

10. **Historical Inquiry Project:** Your student(s) will choose a topic from the reading to learn more about and explore that topic through library visits, museum trips, visiting historical sites, etc.

Visit https://www.nhd.org/how-enter-contest for detailed information on how to put together a historical inquiry project. You may even want to have your students enter the national contest.

How to use this workbook in the classroom

Aunt Phil's Trunk Alaska History Curriculum was created for homeschooling families, but it also can work well in a co-op or classroom setting. Here are some suggestions on how to use this curriculum in a classroom setting. Use what works best for your classroom.

1. **Facts to Know:** The teacher introduces students to the Facts to Know to familiarize the students with terms that they will encounter in the chapter.

2. **Read the chapter:** The teacher can read the chapter aloud while the students follow along in the book. Students also may take turns reading aloud.

3. **Comprehension Questions:** The teacher uses these questions to test the students' comprehension of the chapter. Students should write out the answers in their study guide and the teacher can review the answers with the students in class.

4. **Discussion Questions:** The teacher chooses a few students to answer these questions orally during class. Alternatively, teachers can assign these questions to be completed in essay form individually and answers can be shared during class.

5. **Map Work:** Some chapters will contain a map activity for your students to learn more about the geography of the region that they are learning about. Have your students complete the activity independently.

6. **Enrichment and Online References:** Assign enrichment activities as you see fit.

7. **Daily Review:** Students should review the material for the current unit daily. You can do this by asking review questions orally. Playing review games like Jeopardy or Around the World is a fun way to get your students excited about the material.

8. **Unit Review:** At the end of a unit, your student will complete Unit Review questions and word puzzles in the study guide. Have students review all the unit chapters before completing.

9. **Unit Test:** (Optional) There is an optional test that you can administer to your students after they have completed all the unit work.

10. **Oral Presentation:** (Optional) Assign a 5-minute oral presentation on any topic in the reading. Encourage your student(s) to utilize the additional books and online resources to supplement the information in the textbook. Set aside a classroom day for students to share their presentations.

11. **Historical Inquiry Project:** Your student(s) will choose a topic from the reading to learn more about and explore that topic through library visits, museum trips, visiting historical sites, etc.

Visit https://www.nhd.org/how-enter-contest for detailed information on how to put together a historical inquiry project. You may even want to have your students enter the national contest.

How to grade the assignments

Our rubric grids are designed to make it easy for you to grade your students' essays, oral presentations and enrichment activities. Encourage your students to look at the rubric grid before completing an assignment as a reminder of what an exemplary assignment should include.

You can mark grades for review questions, essay tests and extra credit assignments on the last page of each unit in the student workbook. Use these pages as a tool to help your students track their progress and improve their assignment grades.

Unit Review Questions

Students are given one point for each correct review and fill-in-the-blank question. Mark these points on the last page of each unit in the student workbook.

Essay Test Questions

Students will complete two or more essay questions at the end of each unit. These questions are designed to test your students' knowledge about the key topics of each unit. You can give a student up to 20 points for each essay.

Students are graded on a scale of 1-5 in four categories:

1) Understanding the topic
2) Answering all questions completely and accurately
3) Neatness and organization
4) Grammar, spelling and punctuation

Use the essay rubric grid on page 11 as a guide to give up to 5 points in each category for every essay. Mark these points for each essay on the last page of each Unit Review in the student workbook.

Word Puzzles

Word puzzles that appear at the end of the Unit Reviews count for 3 points, or you can give partial points if the student does not fill in the puzzle completely. Mark these points under the extra category on the last page of each Unit Review in the student workbook.

Enrichment Activities

Most lessons contain an enrichment activity for further research and interaction with the information in the lesson. You can make these optional or assign every activity as part of the lesson. You can use the provided rubric on page 12 to give up to 5 points for each assignment. Mark these points under the extra category on the last page of each Unit Review in the student workbook.

Oral Presentations

You have the option of assigning oral presentations on any topic from the unit as extra credit. If you choose to assign oral presentations, you can use the provided rubric to grade your student on content and presentation skills. Discuss what presentation skills you will be grading your student on before each presentation day.

Some examples of presentation skills you can grade on include:

- Eye contact with the audience
- Proper speaking volume
- Using correct posture
- Speaking clearly

Use the oral presentation rubric grid on page 12 as a guide to give up to 10 points. Mark these points under the extra category on the last page of each Unit Review in the student workbook.

Rubric for Essay Questions

	Beginning 1	Needs Improvement 2	Acceptable 3	Accomplished 4	Exemplary 5
Demonstrates Understanding of the topic	Student's work shows incomplete understanding of the topic	Student's work shows slight understanding of the topic	Student's work shows a basic understanding of the topic	Student's work shows complete understanding of the topic	Student's work demonstrates strong insight about the topic
Answered questions completely and accurately	Student's work did not address all of the questions	Student answered all of the questions with some accuracy	Student answered all questions with close to 100% accuracy	Student answered all questions with 100% accuracy	Student goes beyond the questions to demonstrate knowledge of the topic
Essay is neat and well organized	Student's work is sloppy and unorganized	Student's work is somewhat neat and organized	Student's essay is neat and somewhat organized	Student's work is well organized and neat	Student demonstrates extra care in organizing the essay and making it neat
Essay contains good grammar and spelling	Student's work is poorly written and hard to understand	Student's work contains some grammar, spelling and punctuation mistakes, but not enough to impede understanding	Student's work contains only 1 or 2 grammar, spelling or punctuation errors	Student's work contains no grammar, spelling or punctuation errors	Student's work is extremely well-written

Rubric for Oral Presentations

	Beginning 1	Needs Improvement 2	Acceptable 3	Accomplished 4	Exemplary 5
Preparation	Student did not prepare for the presentation	Student was somewhat prepared for the presentation	Student was prepared for the presentation and addressed the topic	Student was well-prepared for the presentation and addressed important points about the topic	Student prepared an excellent presentation that exhibited creativity and originality
Presentation Skills	Student demonstrated poor presentation skills (no eye contact, low volume, appears disinterested in the topic)	Student made some effort to demonstrate presentation skills (eye contact, spoke clearly, engaged audience, etc.)	Student demonstrated acceptable presentation skills (eye contact, spoke clearly, engaged audience, etc.)	Student demonstrated good presentation skills (eye contact, spoke clearly, engaged audience, etc.)	Student demonstrated strong presentation skills (eye contact, spoke clearly, engaged audience, etc.)

Rubric for Enrichment Activities

	Beginning 1	Needs Improvement 2	Acceptable 3	Accomplished 4	Exemplary 5
	Student's work is incomplete or inaccurate	Student's work is complete and somewhat inaccurate	Student completed the assignment with accuracy	Student's work is accurate, complete, neat and well-organized	Student demonstrates exceptional creativity or originality

UNIT 1: EARLY ALASKA

LESSON 1: UNANSWERED QUESTIONS

FACTS TO KNOW

Phyllis Downing Carlson (Aunt Phil) – Writer and Alaska historian whose research inspired this Alaska history book series
Cook Inlet – Area that stretches from the Gulf of Alaska to Anchorage
Petroglyph – Greek for rock carving
Potlatch – A ceremonial feast where possessions are given away to display wealth or enhance prestige

COMPREHENSION QUESTIONS

1) According to archaeologist Frederica de Laguna, how far back does the ancient Eskimo period go in the Kachemak Bay area? What does she call the phases of Eskimo history in this region?
Frederica de Laguna placed the first phase of Eskimo history as far back as 800 B.C. She divided the Eskimo period into three stages, Kachemak phases I, II and III. (Page 9)

2) Many archeologists and historians have had theories about how long the Tanaina (later called Dena'ina) people were present on the Inlet. What are two of these theories?
Joan Townsend places the beginning of Tanaina occupancy around 100 years before the coming of the Russians in the last quarter of the 18th century. The earliest reference to the Tanaina was in 1762 when a Russian fur trader, Stepan Glotov, was told that the Koniags often traded with the Tanaina. (Page 11)

3) What was the significance of the stones on the Russian River to the Tanaina, according to the Natives at Kenai?
It was reported by Natives at Kenai that stones on the Russian River acted as watchmen when the Tanaina were attacked by the Seward region Eskimos. (Page 12)

4) Why did the Native people of the Cook Inlet region fight against the Russian settlers?
There was much discontent among the Native tribes over their treatment by the Russians. (Pages 11-12)

5) What is the significance of Alaska's petroglyphs? What can they tell us about the Native people of Alaska?

The carvings are in abundance in Southeastern Alaska and are unique because they are associated with salmon streams. Mouths of salmon streams are filled with inscriptions pecked into hard rock like sandstone, slate and granite while good rocks for carving remain bare in villages near those streams. The petroglyphs in this area show how central salmon was to this culture. (Pages 17-18)

DISCUSSION QUESTION

(Discuss this question with your teacher or write your answer in essay form below. Use additional paper if necessary.)

Describe what happened in the "last Indian war in Tyonek."

_____
_____
_____
_____
_____
_____
_____
_____
_____
_____
_____
_____

ENRICHMENT ACTIVITY

The Cook Inlet area that we are studying about is in Southcentral Alaska. Learn more about this region by visiting http://www.akhistorycourse.org/geography/alaskas-location and write a paragraph about what you learned.

TO LEARN MORE

Look for these books at your local library:

The First Americans: Origins, Affinities, and Adaptions. By Laughlin, William S. and Albert B. Harper New York: Gustav Fischer, 1979.

Ancient Men of the Arctic. By Giddings, J.L. New York: Alfred A. Knopf, 1967.
Eskimo Prehistory. By Bandi, Hans-George. Ann E. Keep, translator. College: University of Alaska Press, 1969.

UNIT 1: EARLY ALASKA

LESSON 2: COPING WITH THE UNKNOWN

FACTS TO KNOW

Intermediary – A person who goes between people, groups or entities
Shaman – Medicine man
Sha-E-Dah-Kla – Thought to be the most powerful medicine man in Cook Inlet

COMPREHENSION QUESTIONS

1) <u>Siberia</u> is believed to be the birthplace of shamanism. Shamans acted as intermediaries between <u>the people of the tribe</u> and <u>the spirit world</u>. *(Page 20)*

2) What and when was "Kiyesvilavic"? What happens during the shaman contests?
<u>Kiyesvilavic is the time when the shamans got busy, which included the months of November through January, the short daylight northern season. Shamans would hold contests to pit their prowess against one another.</u> *(Page 20)*

3) What was the shaman's role in a war party?
<u>Every war party included a shaman, who through his supernatural knowledge, warned of danger and pointed out favorable times for attack.</u> *(Page 21)*

4) In healing, the shaman seems to have acted as both <u>paramedic</u> and <u>medical specialist.</u> *(Page 21)*

5) What were the two primary causes of illness recognized by Northern Alaska Eskimo societies?
<u>First, the soul leaving the body, wandering in dreams and failing to return. The second cause was the concept of intrusion, or the driving of some object into the patient's body by a hostile or malevolent shaman.</u> *(Page 21)*

6) What were some of the ways that shamans would heal disease or injury?
One man was badly bleeding from his leg. The shaman took a drum, sang over the wound and talked over it. One shaman operated on a man with stomach problems and extracted the disease using his mouth. Shamans believed that bad spirits were the cause of some disease and would tell the spirits to go home. (Pages 21-26)

DISCUSSION QUESTION

(Discuss this question with your teacher or write your answer in essay form below. Use additional paper if necessary.)

Many of the ideas that Alaska Natives had about the causes of disease and methods of healing are different from modern-day medicine. Explain how they differ using what you read in the chapter and what you know about modern-day medicine in America.

_____
_____
_____
_____
_____
_____
_____
_____
_____
_____
_____

ENRICHMENT ACTIVITY

Much of Chapter 2 was based on miraculous stories that have been passed down for generations. What is one story that has been passed down in your family? Do you have a story about an older relative that may have been passed down from your grandparents or parents? If not, ask one of your relatives for a story. Write down your story in paragraph form.

TO LEARN MORE

You can read more about shamanism by visiting http://www.akhistorycourse.org/alaskas-cultures/shamanism-a-personal-view

You can read more about traditional Native Alaskan remedies and health by visiting http://www.akhistorycourse.org/alaskas-cultures/alaska-natives-and-health

Above: A shaman's rattle, like the one seen here, was used to summon animal and ancestors' spirits to help with healing, sources say.

Below: Tlingit shaman, dressed in hide tunic with mother of pearl buttons, holds a rattle while he kneels by a sick man in the 1800s.

UNIT 1: EARLY ALASKA

LESSON 3: EXPLORERS PLY ALASKA WATERS

FACTS TO KNOW

    Vitus Bering – Danish-born explorer for the Russian Navy/Bering Sea was named after him

    Northwest Passage – A fabled trading route across the top of North America from Europe to Asia

    Aleuts – Native Alaskan group mainly residing in south and southwest Alaska

    Captain James Cook – English explorer who searched for the Northwest Passage

COMPREHENSION QUESTIONS

1) When did European explorers first start coming to Alaska? Who did they find there?
When European explorers rounded the coasts of Alaska in the early 18th century, they discovered the country inhabited by Eskimos in the north, west and Prince William Sound areas; Aleuts in the southwest; Athabascans in the interior and Cook Inlet areas; and Tlingit and Haida Indians in the southeast. (Page 29)

2) In 1728, Danish-born navigator *Vitus Bering*, sailing for the *Russian* Navy of Czar Peter the Great, made his way through the narrow waterway that separates the Seward Peninsula of Alaska from the Chukotka Peninsula to Siberia. What happened during his first voyage? And his second?
During his first voyage, Bering came close to Alaska's coast, but bad weather prevented him from making an official sighting. On the second voyage, he brought an additional ship. The second ship, St. Paul, reached the Prince of Wales Island on July 15, 1741 and Bering's ship, St. Peter, sighted Mount St. Elias and Kayak Island the next day. (Page 29)

3) How did the Russian traders treat the Aleut people?
Russian traders used bribery and coercion, often taking hostages and demanding their ransom to be paid in fur. They depleted the stock of furbearing animals in many areas and killed or enslaved large numbers of Aleuts. (Pages 30, 34)

4) Russia was not the only country to send explorers to Alaska. The *French, Spanish* and *English* governments also were eager to share in Alaska's bounty. *(Page 31)*

5) When did Captain James Cook sail to Alaska? What was he looking for? What important discoveries did he make?
Cook set sail in 1776 aboard his 462-ton Resolution to find the fabled Northwest Passage, a trading route across the top of North America, from Europe to Asia. Cook established that there was no land connection between the Asian and North American continents. He and his expedition also produced maps that set the navigation standard for the next century. (Pages 31-33)

DISCUSSION QUESTION

(Discuss this question with your teacher or write your answer in essay form below. Use additional paper if necessary.)

We learned that explorers came to Alaska from all over the world. What were some of the reasons that the explorers came to Alaska?

_____
_____
_____
_____
_____
_____
_____
_____
_____
_____
_____
_____

MAP ACTIVITY

When Europeans began exploring Alaska in the early 18th-century, they found the land already inhabited by various Native groups. Using the map below and Page 29 in your textbook, write down the name of the Native group the Europeans encountered in each region.

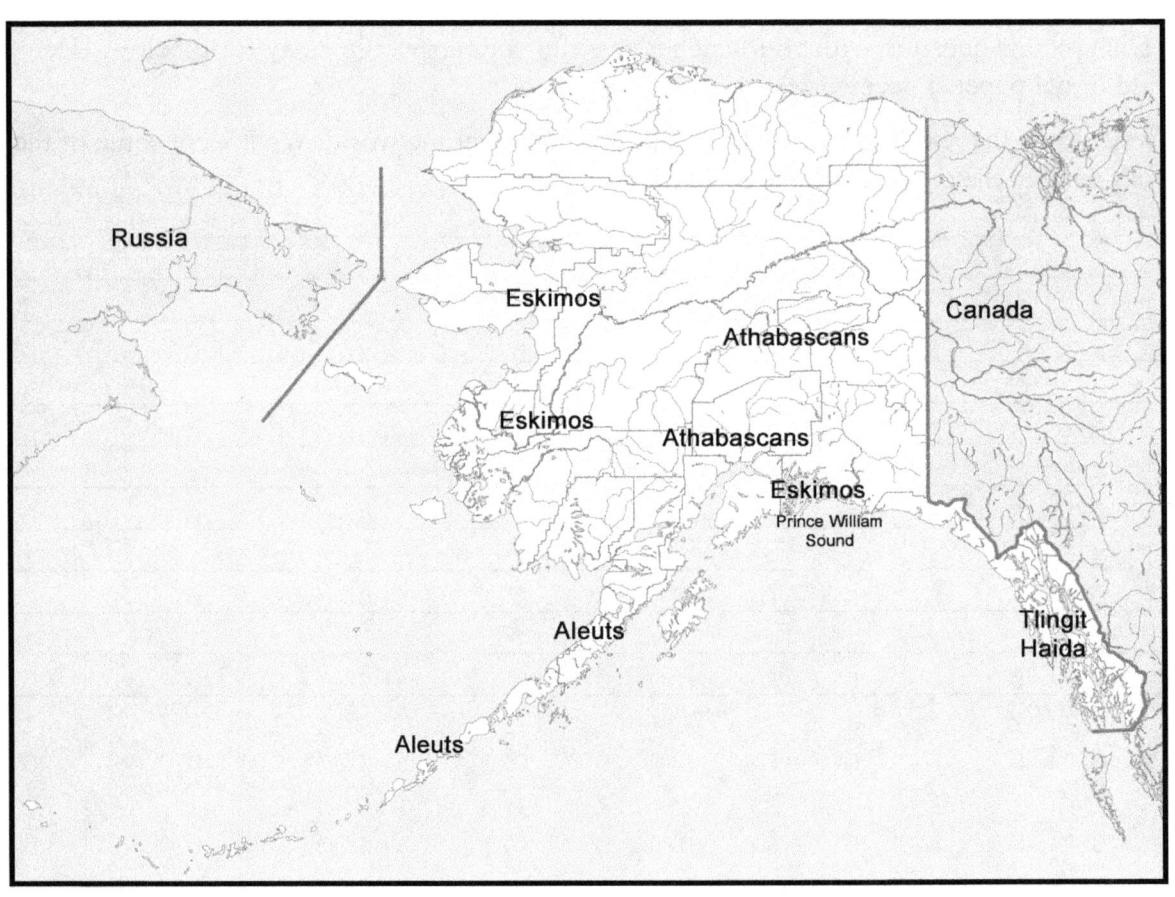

Early Alaska History
Word Scramble Key

1.	trftasiac	artifacts	Objects made by a human being, typically an item of cultural or historical interest.
2.	heiCf	Chief	A leader or ruler of a people or clan.
3.	naSahm	Shaman	A person regarded as having access to, and influence in, the world of good and evil spirits.
4.	ahptoclt	potlatch	A ceremonial feast at which possessions are given away to display wealth or enhance prestige.
5.	mttneeltse	settlement	A place, typically one that previously has been uninhabited, where people establish a community.
6.	uiamk	umiak	An Eskimo open boat made with skin stretched over a wooden frame.
7.	drtaun	tundra	A vast, flat and treeless Arctic region in which the subsoil is permanently frozen.
8.	ucrtelu	culture	The way of life, especially the general customs and beliefs, of a particular group of people.
9.	ecldsanap	landscape	All the visible features of an area of countryside or land.
10.	ogltpepyhr	petroglyph	A carving or inscription on a rock.

UNIT 1: EARLY ALASKA

LESSON 4: WHILE THE UNITED STATES WAS FORMING

FACTS TO KNOW

   Juan Perez – Spanish explorer who discovered Mount Edgecumbe and Shelikof Bay
   Russian-American Company – Government sponsored company that monopolized the fur-trading industry in Alaska
   Alexander Andreevich Baranof – First manager of the Russian-American Company

COMPREHENSION QUESTIONS

For each United States historical event, list which important event was happening in Alaska at or around that time:

1) The Revolutionary War (1775) *Spaniard Juan Perez sailed the west coast of America by order of his government. He, along with Bruno Heceta and Juan Francisco de Bodega y Cuadra, discovered Mount Edgecumbe and Shelikof Bay. (Page 37)*

2) The Second Continental Congress adopted the Declaration of Independence (1776) *Orders were issued by the Spanish to outfit another expedition to continue and complete the discoveries of Perez, although it wasn't until 1779 that the expedition finally set sail. (Page 37)*

3) Eight days after the signing of the Declaration of Independence *Captian James Cook sailed from England on his epic voyage to find the Northwest passage. (Page 37)*

4) The Philadelphia Convention was drawing up the Constitution (1776-1781) *The English, Portuguese, Spanish and French took possession of much of the land in Alaska. (Page 37)*

5) After the defeat of the English at Yorktown and the Articles of Confederation (1781-1783) *Shelikof sailed from Okhotsk to establish a base for colonization in Russian America. (Page 38)*

DISCUSSION QUESTION

(Discuss this question with your teacher or write your answer in essay form below. Use additional paper if necessary.)

From Page 39, "So while the United States was struggling to become a nation after throwing off the yoke of colonialism, Alaska, which later became its northernmost state, was being explored, exploited, and taken over by western nations. Its colonization of the United States was coming to an end."

Explain this quote in your own words. Then share two examples from the chapter to back up this statement.

_____
_____
_____
_____
_____
_____
_____
_____
_____
_____
_____
_____
_____
_____

ENRICHMENT ACTIVITY

Imagine that you are an explorer to Alaska from a distant land. Write your own log entry (journal) about one of your adventures in exploration. What did you see? Who did you meet? What happened?

TO LEARN MORE

You can read more about the Russian explorers to Alaska by visiting http://www.akhistorycourse.org/russias-colony/alaskas-heritage/chapter-3-1-russians-come-to-alaska

You can read more about the beginning of exploration in Alaska by visiting http://www.akhistorycourse.org/russias-colony/the-beginning-of-exploration

UNIT 1: EARLY ALASKA

LESSON 5: ISLAND OF MYSTERY
LESSON 6: EARTHQUAKES FORM LANDSCAPE

Note: Read both chapters 5 and 6 before completing this lesson.

FACTS TO KNOW

Bogoslof – Island created by volcanic activity west of Unalaska/Dutch Harbor
Earthquake – A sudden and violent shaking of the ground, sometimes causing great destruction, as a result of movements within the earth's crust or volcanic action
Landscape – All the visible features of an area of countryside or land

COMPREHENSION QUESTIONS

1) What is the name of the "island of mystery" described in Chapter 5? Why is it called the island of mystery?
The mystery island, named Bogoslof, is composed of black sand that's unstable and shifts with the tide. (Pages 40-41)

2) Describe the emergence of Castle Rock in 1796.
Early in 1796, amid thunder, earthquake and steam, the volcanic island, later called Castle Rock, emerged from the depths of the sea. According to Kriukof, a resident agent of the Russian-American Company, on May 7, a storm came and an island could be seen rising from the waters. (Page 41)

3) Name some animals Lt. George E. Morris Jr. found living on Bogoslof in the 1930s?
Lt. Morris found hundreds of sea lions, gulls, mures and a few other species of birds were the only inhabitants of the land. (Page 42)

4) On what parts of Alaska's landscape can you see evidence of earthquakes?
Alaska's earthquake history has been written on many parts of its landscape, including riverbeds, glaciers and mountains. (Page 44)

5) Southeast Alaska experienced a series of major earthquakes, including one that threatened to wipe out which town on April 2, 1836? What annual tradition did Bishop Veniaminov institute after this earthquake?
On April 2, 1836, an earthquake triggered a series of waves that threatened to wipe out the entire town of Sitka. Bishop Veniaminov ordained that in order to give thanks for the town's salvation, a procession should march through all of Sitka's streets on Annunciation Day. (Pages 44-46)

6) At *Lituya* Bay there is a great "loose joint" in the earth's crust, geologists say. Some of the world's mightiest *peaks* and *glaciers* lie astride it, and when *earthquakes* occur mountains twist, shake and tumble around. *(Page 48)*

7) Uplift and subsidence that accompanied the *Good Friday* earthquake in *1964* affected an area of at least 34,000 square miles. *(Page 48)*

DISCUSSION QUESTION

(Discuss this question with your teacher or write your answer in essay form below. Use additional paper if necessary.)

After reading Chapters 5 and 6, why do you think the earthquakes and volcanic eruptions that we studied are an important part of Alaska's history?

___
___
___
___
___
___
___
___
___
___
___

TO LEARN MORE

You can read more about why the geological history of Alaska is so important by visiting http://www.akhistorycourse.org/geography/alaskas-heritage/chapter-1-1-geological-and-glacial-history

TIME TO REVIEW

Review Chapters 1-6 of your book before moving on to the Unit Review. See how many questions you can answer without looking at your book.

UNIT 1: EARLY ALASKA

REVIEW LESSONS 1-6

Write down what you remember about:

Phyllis Downing Carlson (Aunt Phil) – *Writer and Alaska historian whose research inspired this Alaska history book series*

Cook Inlet – *Area stretching from Gulf of Alaska to Anchorage*

Potlatch – *A ceremonial feast where possessions are given away to display wealth or enhance prestige.*

Shaman – *Medicine man*

Petroglyphs – *Greek for rock carving*

Intermediary – *A person who goes between people, groups or entities*

Vitus Bering – *Danish-born explorer for the Russian Navy/Bering Land Bridge was named after him*

Northwest Passage – *Fabled trading route across the top of North America, from Europe to Asia*

Aleuts – *Native Alaskan group mainly residing in south and southwest Alaska*

Captain James Cook – *English explorer that searched for the Northwest Passage*

Russian-American Company – *Government sponsored company that monopolized the fur-trading industry in Alaska*

Bogoslof – *Island created by volcanic activity west of Unalaska/Dutch Harbor*

Earthquake – *A sudden and violent shaking of the ground, sometimes causing great destruction, as a result of movements within the earth's crust or volcanic action*

Landscape – *All the visible features of an area of countryside or land*

Fill in the blanks:

1) *Frederica de Laguna*, a dedicated archaeologist who carried out a thorough study of the ancient Eskimo culture in the *Kachemak* Bay during the 1930s divided the Eskimo culture in *Kachemak* Bay into three stages that she called *Kachemak phases I, II and III.*

2) Joan Townsend places the beginning of Tanaina (Dena'ina) occupancy around *100* years *before* the coming of the Russians in the last quarter of the 18th-century. When Captain James Cook, in *1778*, described the people he met in what is today known as Cook Inlet, they and their culture strongly resembled some late descriptions of the Tanaina.

3) It was reported by the Natives at Kenai that stones on the Russian River acted as *watchmen* when the Tanaina were attacked by the *Seward region Eskimos*. Nickaffor Alexan, one of the oldtimers at the Indian village Tyonek on the west side of *Cook Inlet*, told Aunt Phil of the last Indian War in his village. It was between the *Tyonek* and *Knik* people.

4) Alaska's *petroglyphs*, Greek for rock carving, are among many enigmas of science. The carvings are in Southeastern Alaska and are unique because they are associated with *salmon streams*, rather than primitive village sites, and always face the sea.

5) *Siberia* is believed to be the birthplace of shamanism. Shamans acted as intermediaries between *the people* and *the unknown*. In healing, the *shaman* seems to have acted as both *paramedic* and *medical specialist*.

6) When *European* explorers rounded the coasts of Alaska in the early *18th* century, they discovered the country inhabited by *Eskimos* in the north, west and Prince William Sound areas; *Aleuts* in the southwest; *Athabascans* in the interior and Cook Inlet areas; and *Tlingit* and *Haida* Indians in the southeast.

7) In 1728, Danish-born navigator *Vitus Bering*, sailing for the *Russian* Navy of Czar Peter the Great, made his way through the narrow waterway that separates the Seward Peninsula of Alaska from the Chukotka Peninsula to Siberia.

8) Russia was not the only country to send explorers to Alaska. The *French, Spanish* and *English* governments also were eager to share in Alaska's bounty.

9) Captain *James Cook* set sail in *1776* aboard his ship *Resolution* to find the fabled *Northwest Passage* from *Europe* to the *Orient*.

10) The mystery island, named *Bogoslof*, is composed of *black sand* that's unstable and shifts with the tide. Its first recorded eruption occurred in *the mid-1790s.*

11) In *1958*, all heck broke lose at Yakutat and *Lituya Bay*. At about 10:17 p.m. an *earthquake* began to shake a vast area of Southeastern Alaska and northern British Columbia.

12) The story of Alaska's *earthquakes* is written in our *landscape*. The evidence attests to *nature's* awesome power.

Early Alaska History
Word Search Key

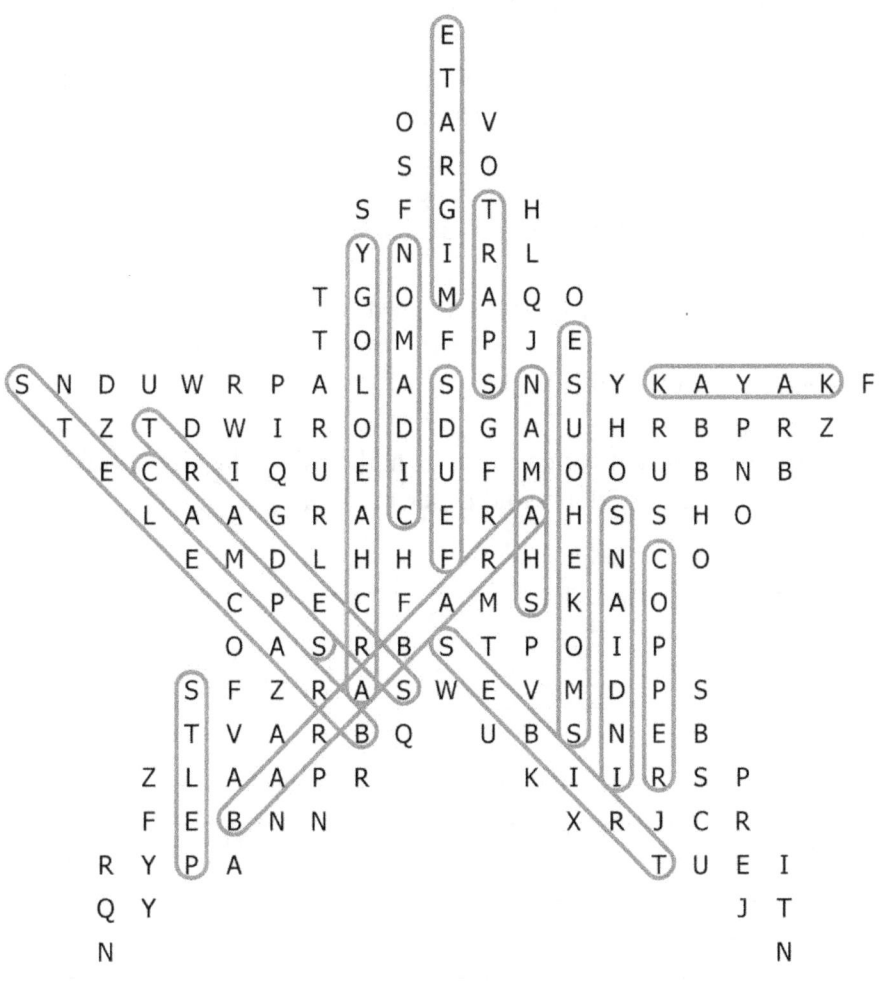

Words

ARCHAEOLOGY	COPPER	MIGRATE	SMOKEHOUSE
BARABARA	FEUDS	NOMADIC	TRADERS
BRACELETS	INDIANS	PELTS	TRAPS
CAMPS	KAYAK	SHAMAN	TRIBES

UNIT 1: EARLY ALASKA

UNIT TEST

Choose *two* of the following questions to answer in paragraph form. Use as much detail as possible to completely answer the question.

1) Aunt Phil had many unanswered questions about Alaska's history. What was one of her unanswered questions? Describe one or more theories that may answer this question.

2) Describe the impact of the Russian fur traders settling in Alaska. How did they treat the Natives? How did the Natives treat the Russians?

3) Why did explorers come to Alaska from all over the world? Give at least one example of an explorer that came to Alaska. When did he come to Alaska and why? What happened when he got to Alaska?

4) What significance did the volcanic eruptions and earthquakes have on Alaska's history? Name one of these events and describe the impact it had on the area.

TEACHER NOTES ABOUT THIS UNIT

UNIT 2: LITTLE-KNOWN STORIES

LESSON 7: NATIVES ATTACK RUSSIAN FORTS

FACTS TO KNOW

Tlingit Indians – Members of an American Indian people of the coasts and islands of southeastern Alaska, including Sitka, and adjacent British Columbia

Nulato – Athabascan village on the Yukon River/name means "dog salmon camp"

Petr Malakhov – Assistant navigator for Russian-American Company who saw Nulato's trading potential

New Archangel – Name of the Russian settlement in southeast Alaska after Alexander Baranof rebuilt it in 1804 (later known as Sitka)

COMPREHENSION QUESTIONS

1) In 1802, which group attacked the Russian settlement in Sitka while Alexander Baranof was away? Why did they attack?
Tlingit Indians attacked the Russian settlement in Sitka. They attacked because they wanted their land back. (Pages 50-51)

2) When did Baranof return to the settlement? What did he bring with him? For what purpose?
In April 1804, Baranof returned to Sitka with four small ships, 300 canoes, and a crew of 121 Russians and 800 Aleuts. He retook the fort, erected a stronger stockade and buildings and renamed the settlement New Archangel. (Page 52)

3) When did Nulato become a trading center for the Russians? Who noticed the trading potential of this area? Did the villagers want to trade with the Russians?
Petr Malakhov, assistant navigator for the Russian-American Company saw Nulato's trading potential when he observed coastal Eskimos come to the village offering seal and whale oil, tobacco and copper spearheads in trade. The villagers welcomed the trade with the Russians. (Page 52)

4) For _12_ years, the Russians traded peacefully with the village of _Nulato_, which means "dog salmon camp." But on a dark Sunday, February 16, _1851_, that all changed when the _Koyukon Indians_ came to town.

5) Describe what happened during the massacre.
A band of Koyukuk Indians led by a shaman, Red Shirt, stuffed bundles of grass in the trading post chimney to smoke out the Russian trader. The men fled the post and were hit with arrows. The Koyukuk warriors killed all the people in the village except for a small boy and girl. (Pages 53-54)

6) What are some of the theories that have arisen to explain the massacre?
Many theories have arisen to explain the massacre, including Russian oppression and brutal treatment of the Indians, rivalries between shamans, the peremptory tone of Lt. Bernard when addressing the Koyukuk chief, or perhaps a dispute over local trade. (Page 54)

DISCUSSION QUESTION

(Discuss this question with your teacher or write your answer in essay form below. Use additional paper if necessary.)

In his book, *On the Edge of Nowhere*, Jimmy Huntington wrote about the trading process of his Native people. Describe this process.

_____
_____
_____
_____
_____
_____
_____

ENRICHMENT ACTIVITY

Download the Russian American Reader at http://www.akhistorycourse.org/docs/russian_american_book7.pdf

Read the letters between Russia and Kodiak on pages 4-10, and then write a paragraph describing what you learned about the Russian-American Company.

TO LEARN MORE

Read more about the Russian colonization of Alaska by visiting http://www.akhistorycourse.org/docs/russian_american_book7.pdf

Look for this book at your local library:
Kodiak and Afognak Life, 1868-1870. Richard A. Pierce. Kingston, Ontario, Canada: The Limestone Press, 1981.

UNIT 2: LITTLE-KNOWN STORIES

LESSON 8: WOODY ISLAND'S ICY PAST

FACTS TO KNOW

Woody Island – Small island a couple miles off the city of Kodiak
Lake Tanignak – 40-acre lake on Woody Island
Barabara – A sod or turf hut built partly or wholly underground
Tione – Chief

COMPREHENSION QUESTIONS

1) Woody Island is a place of many of Alaska's firsts. What are some of those firsts? Why did these firsts happen here?
The first horses in Alaska were brought here, the first road was constructed, the first iron rails were put in and the first field of oats was sown. And they were all put in place to support one thing: a sawmill, so the residents could start what many people called "Alaska's Wackiest Industry," selling ice. (Page 58)

2) Why was Alaska a prime area for selling ice to California? What part of Alaska did the first shipment come from? How much did that shipment sell for?
Ice sent from Boston via Cape Horn was very expensive and not enough could be supplied to meet the demand. Alaska was closer. The first shipment of ice was sent from Sitka and sold for about $75 a ton in San Francisco. (Page 58)

3) Between _1852_ and _1859_, more than _7,000_ tons of ice was shipped as far south as _Central_ and _South America_, bringing at first _$75_ a ton. Later the price fell to _$7_ a ton as _quantity_ increased. *(Page 60)*

4) In the early 1850s, artificial ice machines were invented, but they didn't sell very well. Why not? What did the ice machine manufacturer do to try to stifle competition?
The machines were expensive and few people could afford them. In order to stifle competition, the ice machine manufacturer offered to pay a set sum every year to the Alaska ice company not to ship the ice it chipped out of Lake Tanignak. (Page 60)

5) When was the end of the ice industry in Alaska? Why did it end?
The end of the ice industry came when the Southern Pacific Railroad was built to the coast, making it feasible to ship natural ice from the Sierras into San Francisco, and when artificial ice was invented the price was forced too low to justify Alaska expenses. (Page 63)

DISCUSSION QUESTION

(Discuss this question with your teacher or write your answer in essay form below. Use additional paper if necessary.)

Describe what life was like on Woody Island for the Native workers.

LEARN MORE

Read more about the Alaska Ice Company and other economic activities that Russians took part in by visiting http://www.akhistorycourse.org/russias-colony/alaskas-heritage/chapter-3-6-other-economic-activity

UNIT 2: LITTLE-KNOWN STORIES

LESSON 9: LAST SHOT OF THE CIVIL WAR

FACTS TO KNOW

Shenandoah – An English-built Confederate vessel used to disrupt northern commerce on the high seas

Appomattox – Place where the American Civil War ended in April 1865

Confederate – A supporter of the Confederate States of America during the American Civil War, 1861-1865

Yankee – Slang term for a member of the United States of America by the Confederates (also refers to a person who lives in, or is from, the United States)

COMPREHENSION QUESTIONS

1) What was "the last shot of the civil war," and when did it happen?
Not knowing the war had ended in Appomattox 74 days earlier, the commander of an English-built Confederate vessel named the Shenandoah fired upon several whalers near St. Lawrence Island on June 22, 1865. (Page 64)

2) Why was the *Shenandoah* in the Bering Sea of Alaska?
The Shenandoah was one of several ships used by the Confederates to disrupt Yankee commerce on the high seas. (Page 64)

3) The Shenandoah covered _58,000_ miles and captured _38_ Yankee ships. *(Page 64)*

4) How and when did the crew of the *Shenandoah* learn the war was over?
The Shenandoah sailed down the Aleutian Chain and set a course for the coast of California. On Aug. 2, 1865, just 13 days out of San Francisco, she overtook the English bark Barracouta. That's when the crew learned the war was over. (Page 65)

5) Where and when did the commander and crew of the *Shenandoah* surrender?
On Nov. 6, 1865, the Shenandoah dropped anchor in Mersey off Liverpool, England. The crew hauled her flag down and surrendered her to the British government. (Page 66)

DISCUSSION QUESTION

(Discuss this question with your teacher or write your answer in essay form below. Use additional paper if necessary.)

How do you think America would be different if the Confederates had won the Civil War?

LEARN MORE

Read more about the American Civil War, also called War Between the States, by visiting https://www.britannica.com/event/American-Civil-War

TIME TO REVIEW

Review Chapters 7-9 before moving on to the Unit Review. See how many questions you can answer without looking at your book.

UNIT 2: LITTLE-KNOWN STORIES

REVIEW LESSONS 7-9

Write down what you remember about:

Tlingit Indians – *Members of an American Indian people of the coasts and islands of southeastern Alaska, including Sitka, and adjacent British Columbia*

Petr Malakhov – *Assistant navigator for Russian-American Company who saw Nulato's trading potential*

Nulato – *Athabascan village on the Yukon River/name means "dog salmon camp"*

New Archangel – *Name of the Russian settlement after Baranof rebuilt it in 1804*

Woody Island – *A small island a couple of miles off the city of Kodiak*

Lake Tanignak – *40-acre lake on Woody Island*

Barabara – *A sod or turf hut built partly or wholly underground*

Tione – *Chief*

Shenandoah – *An English-built Confederate vessel used to disrupt northern commerce on the high seas*

Appomattox – *Place where the American Civil War ended in April 1865*

Confederate – *A supporter of the Confederate States of America during the American Civil War, 1861-1865*

Yankee – *Slang term for a member of the United States of America (also refers to a person who lives in, or is from, the United States)*

Fill in the blanks:

1) In the year *1802*, a group of *Tlingit* warriors attacked the Russian settlement while *Alexander Baranof* was away in Kodiak.

2) In April *1804*, *Alexander Baranof* returned to Sitka with four small ships, 300 canoes, and a crew of 121 *Russians* and 800 *Aleuts*. He retook the fort and erected a stronger stockade and buildings and renamed the settlement *New Archangel*.

3) The *Koyukuk* region came to the attention of the rest of the country, too, when in *1851*, *Koyukon* Natives destroyed the Russian fort at *Nulato*.

4) *Nulato* an Athabascan village on the *Yukon* River, became a trading center for the *Russians* when Russian-American Company assistant navigator *Petr Malakhov*, a Creole, traveled from the company's western fur depot in St. Michael up the Yukon River.

5) The *sawmill* established on Woody Island was perhaps unique in commercial enterprises because its main product was *sawdust,* which was needed to preserve *ice*, something abundant in Alaska that *California* wanted.

6) Between *1852* and *1859*, more than *7,000* tons of ice was shipped as far south as *Mexico* and *South America*, bringing at first *$75* a ton. Later the price fell to *$7* a ton as *quantity* increased.

7) The end of the ice industry came when the *Southern Pacific Railroad* was built to the coast, making it feasible to ship natural ice form the Sierras into San Francisco, and when *artificial ice* was invented the price was forced too low to justify Alaska expenses.

8) Not knowing that the American Civil War had ended in Appomattox *74* days earlier, the commander of an English-built *Confederate* vessel named *the Shenandoah* fired upon several whalers near *St. Lawrence* Island on June 22, *1865*.

9) After learning the war had ended, the commander and crew took the Confederate ship to *England* where they surrendered on *November 6, 1865*.

Early Alaska History
Crossword Puzzle

Read Across and Down clues and fill in blank boxes that match numbers on the clues

Across
1. A ship or large boat
2. Country in which the *Shenandoah* surrendered in November 1865
4. Also known as The War Between the States
7. Supporter of the Confederate States of America during American Civil War
8. Small pieces of glass, stone or similar material used in decoration and trading
9. People who buy and sell goods
11. A brutal slaughter of people
12. Alaska Native group that attacked the Russian fort at Mikhailovsk
15. A barrier formed from upright wooden posts or stakes as a defense against attack
16. Frozen water
20. Lake where residents of Woody Island chipped ice for shipping
21. Drink that workers received every day when working at Woody Island ice business
22. Slang term for a member of the United States of America
24. The Russian settlement in Southeast Alaska called New Archangel later became known as this town
25. Woody Island had one of these to saw logs into lumber and sawdust
26. A building designed to be defended from attack
27. Animal skin, fur and all

Down
1. Small communities or groups of houses or huts in rural areas
3. Place where the American Civil War ended in April 1865
5. Village name that means "dog salmon camp"
6. A person who fights in battles and is known for having courage and skill
8. A sod or turf hut built partially or wholly underground
10. A sum of money or other payment demanded or paid for the release of a prisoner
13. A large body of ice that moves slowly and spreads outward on a land surface
14. Name of island where the residents worked in an ice business in the mid-1800s
15. Red Shirt was one of these
17. First manager of the Russian-American Company
18. The basic monetary unit of Russia
19. A narrow, keel-less boat with pointed ends, propelled by paddles
23. Another word for Chief

Early Alaska History
Crossword Puzzle Key

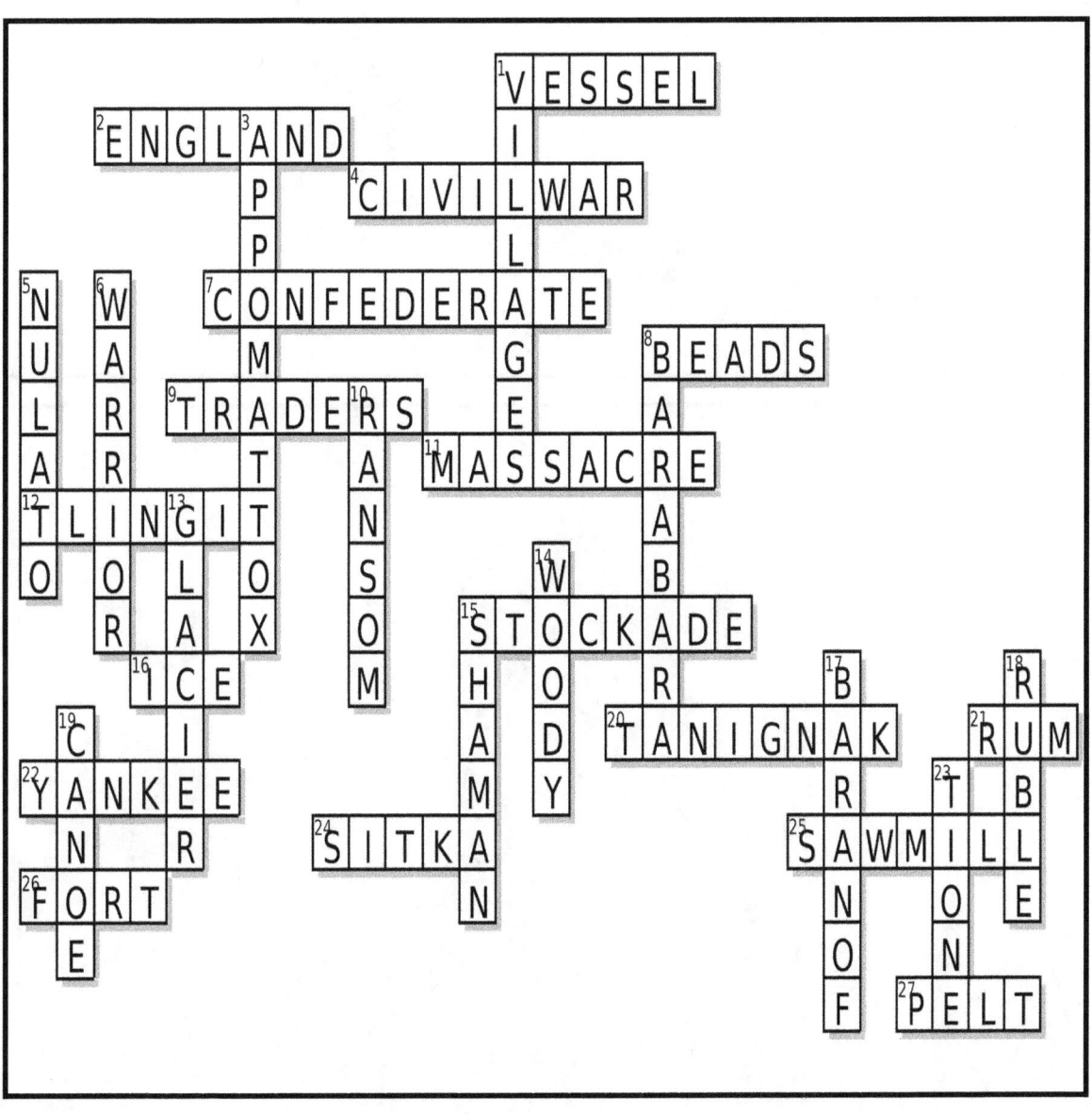

Courtesy Alaska State Library

Courtesy Alaska State Library

Fur became a hot commodity for eary fur traders in Alaska. The Native people had used animal fur and skins for clothing, shelter and other items long before Russian fur traders arrived, as seen in the photos on Page 38.

But fur, and later ice, were not the only commodities that early traders in Alaska exploited. The photo below shows how white whalers and traders cleaned pieces of baleen, a filter-feeder system inside the mouths of baleen whales, during the 1800s to ship to eager buyers in the Lower 48.

Baleen was used much as plastic is used today. Fashionable ladies wore corsets made from baleen to compress their waistlines. One typical corset advertisement from the 1800s proudly proclaimed, "Real Whalebone Only Used."

It also was used for collar stays, buggy whips and toys. Its flexibility led it to be used as the springs in early typewriters, too.

The comparison to plastic is apt. Think of common items which today might be made of plastic, and it's likely that similar items in the 1800s would have been made of whalebone.

Courtesy Alaska State Library

UNIT 2: LITTLE-KNOWN STORIES

UNIT TEST

Choose *two* of the following questions to answer in paragraph form. Use as much detail as possible to completely answer the question.

1) What was the impact of Russian colonization on Alaska's history? Include specific examples.

2) Describe one of the Native attacks on Russian forts as written in Chapter 7 in as much detail as possible. Why did this attack occur?

3) Summarize "Alaska's Wackiest Industry" from start to finish. How did it start and where? What competition did it face? How did it end?

4) What was "the last shot of the civil war"? What happened? Who was involved?

TEACHER NOTES ABOUT THIS UNIT

UNIT 3: ALASKA BECOMES U.S. POSSESSION

LESSON 10: SEWARD'S FOLLY TURNS INTO TREASURE

FACTS TO KNOW:

William H. Seward – U.S. Secretary of State who negotiated with Russia for the purchase of Alaska

Edouard de Stoecki – Russian ambassador who negotiated with Seward to sell Alaska to America

General Jeff Davis – U.S. general that took possession of Alaska from the Russians in 1867

Sitka – The town in Southeast Alaska where the Russian governor of Alaska formally transferred ownership of Alaska to the United States

COMPREHESION QUESTIONS

1) What value did U.S. Secretary of State William H. Seward find in Alaska?
Seward believed that the purchase of Alaska would give the United States more of a military presence in the North Pacific. He recognized all that Russia had built in Alaska and believed that America should build outposts there to expand to the very end of the North American border to establish monuments of the civilization of the United States to the world. (Pages 67-70)

2) When did America sign a treaty to purchase Alaska? What were the terms of the deal between the United States and Russia? When did the U.S. take possession of Alaska?
The treaty was signed in May 1867. The Russians wanted "a cash payment of $7 million, with an additional $200,000 on condition that the cession should be free and unencumbered by any reservations, privileges, franchises or possessions by any associated companies, corporate or incorporate, Russian or any other." General Jeff Davis took possession of Alaska in October 1867. (Pages 68-71)

3) Many Americans, including legislators, thought that it was a bad idea to purchase Alaska. Why?
Many Americans had very little information about Alaska. They believed that it was barren and worthless. Some believed the only products in Alaska were "icebergs and polar bears." (Pages 69-70)

4) What did the U.S. do shortly after taking possession of Alaska? How did the transfer affect Sitka?
Once the transfer of Alaska to the United States from Russia was finalized, the Americans

lost no time converting the small seaport village of Sitka into a hot spot of capitalism. New shops, tenpin alleys, drinking saloons and a restaurant were opened. There were negotiations for the purchases of the property of the Russian-American Company. (Pages 73-74)

5) What happened on April 14, 1865, that could have prevented the United States from purchasing Alaska?
John Wilkes Booth recruited Lewis Paine to kill Seward on April 14 at approximately 10:15 p.m. to coincide with Booth's attack on President Lincoln. Paine did not succeed in killing Seward, but seriously injured him with a Bowie knife, including a serious wound to his right cheek. (Pages 79-81)

DISCUSSION QUESTIONS

(Discuss this question with your teacher or write your answer in essay form below. Use additional paper if necessary.)

How did the Russian population react to the purchase of Alaska? Did they welcome the incoming Americans? How did the Native people of Alaska react? *(Pages 72-75)*

BONUS QUESTION

What do you think would have happened to Alaska if William H. Seward had been killed by the Confederate assassin? Do you think Alaska would still be part of Russia? If so, what effect would that have had on the United States today?

ENRICHMENT ACTIVITY

U.S. Secretary of State William Seward saw the value of Alaska to the United States when many Americans did not. Imagine that you are Secretary Seward. Write a persuasive letter to one of your friends that has doubts about your reasons for wanting to purchase Alaska. Address the doubts that many Americans had about the value of Alaska.

TO LEARN MORE

Read more about the Russian sale of Alaska by visiting http://www.akhistorycourse.org/russias-colony/the-sale-of-russian-america

Look for this book at your local library:
Lady Franklin Visits Sitka, Alaska, 1870. DeArmond, R.N., editor. Anchorage: Alaska Historical Society, 1981.

Courtesy Alaska State Library

The U.S. Army took over the Russian-American Company administrative office building in Sitka, seen here, once Alaska was officially transferred to America on Oct. 18, 1867.

UNIT 3: ALASKA BECOMES U.S. POSSESSION

LESSON 11: MYTH SURROUNDS ALASKA PURCHASE

FACTS TO KNOW:

Czar Alexander II – Russian leader who sent the Russian fleet to America in 1863
President Abraham Lincoln – The 16th President of the United States
American Civil War – A civil war fought from 1861-1865 between the Union and the Confederate States (southern states that seceded in order to prevent President Abraham Lincoln from outlawing slavery in their states)

COMPREHENSION QUESTIONS

1) How much did the United States pay for Alaska? Why did some people think that the purchase price was considerably less?
The United States paid Russia $7.2 million for Alaska. Some people think that this amount included payment to Russia to sail to America to show support for the Northern cause during the Civil War. (Pages 82-83)

2) Was President Abraham Lincoln happy about the arrival of the Russian fleet in America during 1863? Why or why not?
President Lincoln welcomed the morale boost that the Russian fleet brought with its arrival in New York City. Although the Union had defeated the south at Gettysburg, the cost in human lives was high and morale was low. The arrival of the fleet meant hope for the Union. (Pages 86, 88)

3) Why did Britain withdraw its support for the Union? Why was neutrality on the Civil War in the best interest of Britain? Why was neutrality in the best interest of France?
The Britain ruling class wanted to see an end to slavery. But Lincoln abandoned that idea at first in order to keep Southern border states in the Union. Britain's possessions in America were better protected in a divided America. France openly negotiated with the Confederates and Mexico. These interests were protected best by the United States' inability to divert attention from the war. (Page 87)

4) How did New Yorkers welcome the Russian fleet on November 5, 1863? What was said about Czar Alexander II at the event?
On November 5, New Yorkers gave the Russians a ball at the Academy of Music. It was a very important affair attended by leading society people. During all of the balls and banquets, each country toasted the other. Alexander was hailed as the emancipator of the serfs and the friend of America. (Pages 88-89)

5) Historical records show that the United States inquired about purchasing Alaska long before the Civil War. When were the first inquires made into purchasing Alaska and by whom? Why didn't the U.S. purchase Alaska at that point? <u>Secretary of State William Marcy and William Gwin, Democratic Congressman from Mississippi, inquired as early as 1843 whether the Russian colony was for sale. William Gwin, then a senator under President James Buchanan, held several meetings with the Russian minister to negotiate the purchase in 1859. The U.S. offered $5 million. Prince Gortschakof sent a telegram stating that the sum was inadequate.</u> *(Pages 90-91)*

DISCUSSION QUESTION

(Discuss this question with your teacher or write your answer in essay form below. Use additional paper if necessary.)

What two-fold purpose did Czar Alexander sending the Russian fleet to America accomplish? *(Page 90)*

_____
_____
_____
_____
_____
_____
_____
_____
_____
_____
_____
_____
_____
_____
_____

ENRICHMENT ACTIVITY

Read this article http://www.akhistorycourse.org/governing-alaska/after-the-purchase-of-alaska and answer this question:

What did you learn about the Native people's views on the United States purchase of Alaska? Write your answer in paragraph form.

TO LEARN MORE

Read more about the American contact with Russian America by visiting http://www.akhistorycourse.org/russias-colony/alaskas-heritage/chapter-3-10-american-contact-with-russian-america

UNIT 3: ALASKA BECOMES U.S. POSSESSION

LESSON 12: AMERICANS FLOCK NORTH

FACTS TO KNOW:

Wrangell – Third-oldest community in Alaska and home of one of the first U.S. Army posts in Alaska
Unalaska – The largest town of the Aleutian islands
Census – The process of acquiring data about the members of a specific population
Russian Orthodox Church – Religious denomination of the Russians that settled in Alaska

COMPREHENSION QUESTIONS

1) Name some of the reasons that Americans were eager to go to Alaska? What area did many of them travel to?
Americans were eager to engage in trade and commerce. Most of them went to Sitka. *(Page 93)*

2) When *Ivan Petroff* took the first United States Census in *1880*, he counted *33,426* people in the colony. His report provided an abundance of information about Alaska's *resources* and geography. *(Page 96)*

3) When Americans arrived in Alaska, what new settlements did they establish? What industries became important as a result of these new settlements?
Two of these settlements were the Southeastern communities of Juneau and Douglas, which both began as gold-mining camps in 1880 and 1881. Commercial fishing started growing in importance. Many towns, like Ketchikan, started out as fishing villages. *(Pages 96-97)*

4) What became the leading industry in Alaska after the decline of fur at the turn of the century?
By the turn of the century, commercial fishing was the leading industry as the fur industry declined. *(Page 97)*

5) Who was Saint Innocent of Alaska? What significant things did he do in Alaska?
After arriving in Unalaska in 1824, Father Ivan Veniaminov helped spread the Russian Orthodox doctrine to the Aleutians. He taught Natives in their own dialect, Aleutian Fox, after creating an alphabet and translating textbooks and parts of the Bible. He wrote down his observations of Aleut life and recorded Native legends and history. He is now known in the Orthodox Church as Saint Innocent of Alaska. (Page 98)

DISCUSSION QUESTION

(Discuss this question with your teacher or write your answer in essay form below. Use additional paper if necessary.)

As its population grew, several religious groups flooded Alaska. Name one of these groups. What Native people did this religious group serve? What important things did this group do? *(Pages 97-99)*

_____
_____
_____
_____
_____
_____
_____
_____
_____
_____
_____
_____
_____
_____

ENRICHMENT ACTIVITY

History is made up of numerous cause-and-effect relationships. No historical event happens in isolation. Part of historical study is learning how people, places, movements and events are interrelated. Consider what you have learned thus far about the history of Alaska. Write down five cause-and-effect relationships that you notice from your reading. Example: When the United States purchased Alaska in 1867, Americans flocked to Alaska for new economic opportunity.

TO LEARN MORE

Read more about the population and settlements of Alaska after the U.S. purchase by visiting http://www.akhistorycourse.org/americas-territory/population-and-settlements

The Sitka Home Mission, established by Presbyterian missionary Sheldon Jackson and shown above in 1886-1887, served as the education center for Alaska Native children in and around Sitka after Alaska became a U.S. possession in 1867.

The slate tablet shown below was used by a 4-year-old boy who wrote, in chalk, "The book is on the box. It is a big hat. It is my book." He also drew pictures of various items, including a goblet, which was probably a very new word in his vocabulary.

Alaska Purchase
Crossword Puzzle

Read Across and Down clues and fill in blank boxes that match numbers on the clues

Across

2   The Russian admiral who sailed the Russian fleet into New York Harbor in 1863
4   This man took possession of Alaska from the Russians in October 1867
7   Department of U.S. Government that first oversaw Alaska affairs
8   A position usable as a base for further advance
11 The action of becoming larger or more extensive
17 A person who is among the first to explore or settle a new country or area
18 An act of moving something or someone to another place
20 An item of property; something belonging to one
21 The formal giving up of rights, property or territory
22 19th-century doctrine that believed expansion of the United States was both justified and inevitable
23 A person or company involved in wholesale trade
27 Lack of good sense; foolishness
28 Russian Ambassador who brokered Alaska purchase with America
29 The state of not supporting or helping either side in a conflict
31 He took the first U.S. Census for Alaska in 1880
33 Largest town on Aleutian islands and place where the Methodist Church came in 1890
35 The man who negotiated the purchase of Alaska from the Russians
36 This village was first named Mamterillermiut, meaning "Smokehouse People"
38 When the 13 colonies that became the United States came together, they formed this
39 A card game played by William Seward, usually for two pairs of players
40 The process of acquiring data about the members of a specific population
41 The emotional or mental condition of those fighting during the American Civil War with respect to confidence and loyalty
42 The largest group of naval vessels under one commander

Down

1   Russian general who submitted contingency plan for the weak Russian navy in 1863
3   The capacity to have an effect on the character, development or behavior of something
5   A person who serves in an army
6   People sent by a church into an area to carry on evangelism or other activities
9   Man who attempted to assassinate Secretary of State Seward in 1865
10 The formal activities conducted on some solemn or important public or state occasion
12 The action of buying something
13 Third-oldest community in Alaska and home of one of Alaska's first U.S. Army posts
14 A Native who became one of the most influential and capable missionaries in Alaska
15 A person from the same country or region as someone else
16 Place in Sitka where the official transfer of Alaska to America occurred
19 A person who unlawfully occupies an uninhabited building or unused land
24 U.S. President at the time of Alaska purchase from Russia
25 Forecast an uncertain event

Alaska Purchase
Crossword Puzzle Key

Down (continued)
26 Chief of Klukwan who gave William H. Seward a special blanket when Seward visited southeast Alaska after the Alaska purchase.
30 A formally concluded and ratified agreement between countries
32 This became the leading industry in Alaska as the fur industry declined
34 U.S. Senator who supported Alaska purchase
36 Type of knife the would-be assassin used when attacking Secretary of State Seward
37 Place where ceremony to transfer Alaska to Russia was held
41 A widely held but false belief or idea

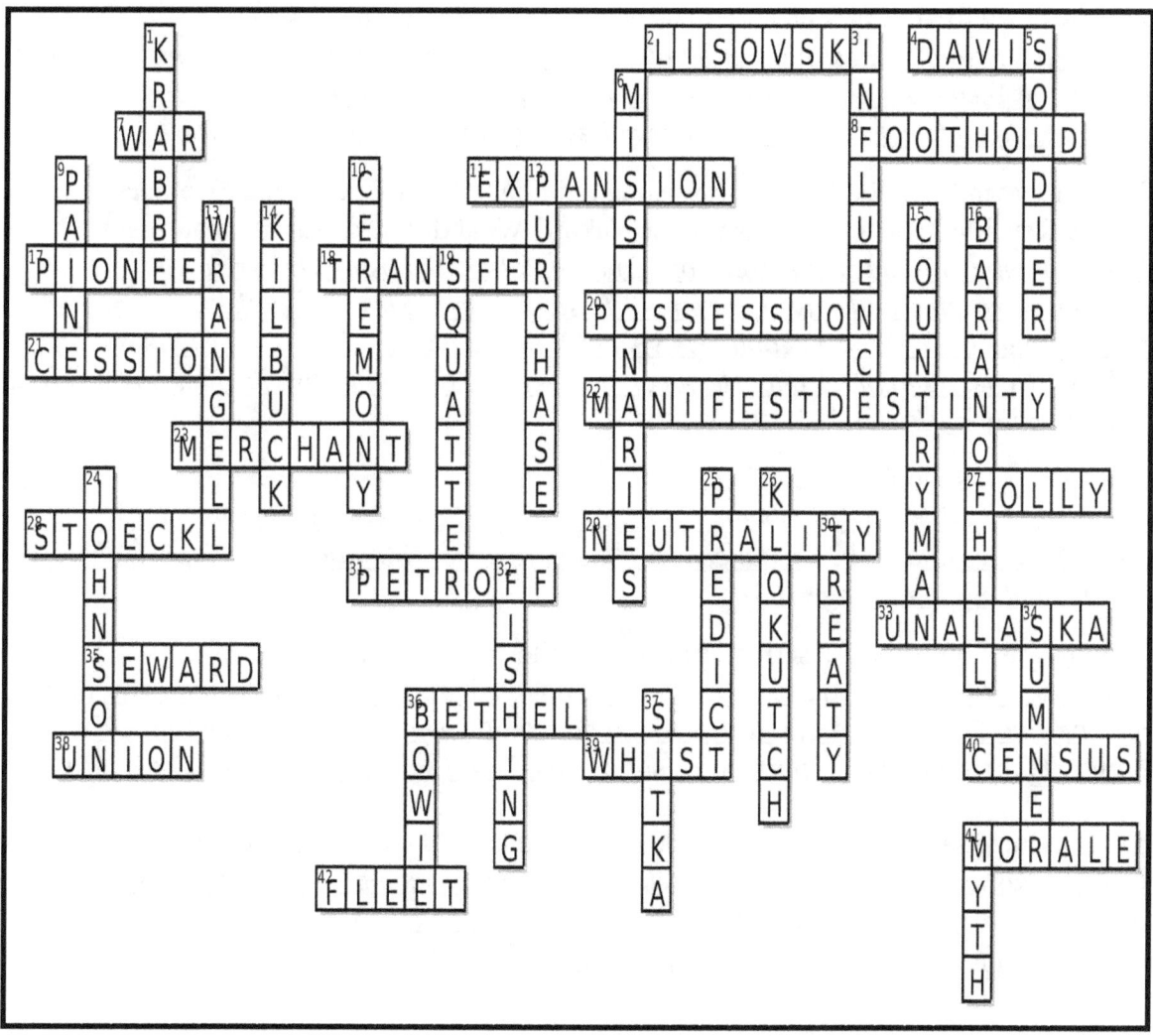

55

UNIT 3: ALASKA BECOMES U.S. POSSESSION

LESSON 13: APOSTLE TO THE NORTH

FACTS TO KNOW:

Fort Yukon – A trading post established by Alexander Murray
William Carpenter Bompas – English missionary and teacher in the Yukon
Miner – A person who extracts ore, coal or other minerals from the earth
George Washington Carmack – One of the men who discovered gold along Rabbit Creek, later named Bonanza, that started the Klondike Gold Rush

COMPREHENSION QUESTIONS

1) How did William Carpenter Bompas begin his mission to the Yukon?
During a missionary meeting in England, Bompas learned of the need for a missionary to help in the Yukon where Rev. Robert McDonald, a pioneer missionary, was ill. His heart was touched and he volunteered to relieve Rev. McDonald. (Pages 100-101)

2) After leaving London in 1865, how long did it take William Carpenter Bompas to relieve Rev. McDonald of his post in the Yukon? What did he do during that time?
It took Bompas 178 days to travel from London to Fort Simpson. He arrived on Christmas morning and stayed there until Easter. He spent his time at the fort studying the language of the Native people. He visited Native camps and spent time with a band of Eskimos traveling to the Arctic. He vaccinated more than 500 Natives against smallpox at Fort Vermillion. (Pages 101-103)

3) Describe Bishop Bompas' wife.
The daughter of an English doctor, Charlotte was raised in Italy, where she had enjoyed elegant parties and had even danced with the king at her first ball. Full of spirit, she was artistic and musical. (Page 103)

4) Why was Fort Yukon described as, "a half mile from the ends of the earth"?
Fort Yukon was about three miles upstream from the mouth of the Porcupine River and well beyond the Arctic Circle. It was so isolated that when the commander shipped a cargo of furs to London, reports were not received until seven years later. (Page 105)

5) What important discovery was made on the banks of the Klondike River in 1896?
George Washington Carmack, along with several Native companions, discovered gold along its banks in 1896. This famous discovery electrified the world and brought thousands into the Yukon to seek precious metal. (Page 106)

DISCUSSION QUESTION

(Discuss this question with your teacher or write your answer in essay form below. Use additional paper if necessary.)

Bishop Bompas and Reverend McDonald spent a lot of time studying the languages of the Native people. Reverend McDonald required his new clergy to spend at least four hours a day in language study. Why was this important? What do you think this meant to the Native people that they served? *(Page 103)*

TO LEARN MORE

Read more about the Yukon River and its people by visiting http://www.akhistorycourse.org/interior-alaska/the-yukon-river-and-its-people

MAP ACTIVITY

Show the location of the following:

1) Arctic Ocean
2) Arctic Circle
3) Yukon region
4) Yukon River
5) Klondike River
6) Bering Sea
7) Gulf of Alaska

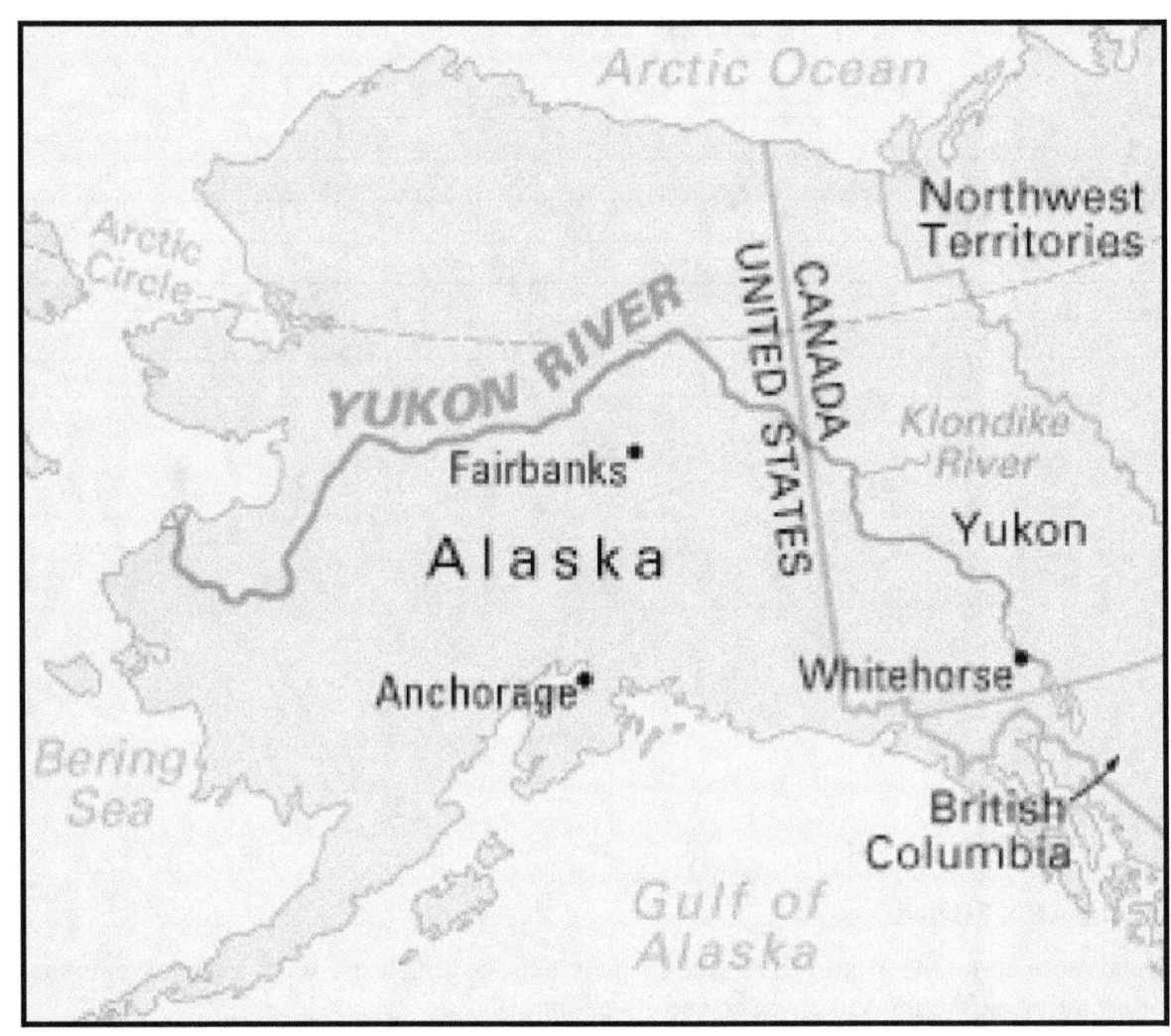

UNIT 3: ALASKA BECOMES U.S. POSSESSION

LESSON 14: ALASKA'S MYSTERIOUS FIRST CENSUS-TAKER

FACTS TO KNOW:

Ivan Petroff – Alaska's first census taker
Territory – An area of land under the authority of a ruler or state
Bidarka – A boat covered in animal skins used by Native people of Alaska

COMPREHENSION QUESTIONS

1) Review Time: In Lesson 12, we learned the definition of a census. Define census.
A census is the process of acquiring data about the members of a population. (Lesson 12 Facts to Know)

2) Why was Ivan Petroff chosen to take the Alaska census in 1880? Why was this a controversial choice?
Ivan Petroff was appointed to take the 1880 census soon after testifying before the Senate Committee on Territories concerning civil government in Alaska. He had a reputation as an authority on Alaska. He was a controversial choice because he deserted the military three times and passed off another journalist's work as his own. (Page 113)

3) How did Ivan Petroff travel to take the census? What obstacles did he encounter?
He traveled by boats, sleds and umiaks. No one knew how large the territory of Alaska was, and there were no roads, only a few Native trails. Travel by water also was at a minimum. A mail steamer reached Sitka only once a month, and other than a few revenue cutters and Native bidarkas, canoes and umiaks, there were few sailing vessels. (Pages 111-112)

4) Name some of the people groups that were recorded on the 1880 census.
Caucasians, Creoles, Inuit, Aleut, Tinneh, Tlingets and Haidas. (Page 112)

5) What two important books did Ivan Petroff contribute to?
Ivan Petroff wrote much of "History of Alaska, 1730-1885" by Hubert Howe Bancroft. After taking the 1880 census, he wrote "Report on the Population, Industries and Resources of Alaska," which was based upon the knowledge he gained while taking the 1880 census. (Page 115)

DISCUSSION QUESTION

(Discuss this question with your teacher or write your answer in essay form below. Use additional paper if necessary.)

What can we learn about Alaska in 1880 from reading what was recorded on the census? Why is this information important? *(Page 115)*

_____
_____
_____
_____
_____
_____
_____
_____
_____
_____
_____
_____
_____
_____
_____
_____
_____
_____
_____

ENRICHMENT ACTIVITY

Imagine that you are in charge of taking the census for your classroom, family, church group or sports team. Write a list of data about the people in your group. You can track gender, age, ethnicity, occupation, city of residence and any other item that you would like to include in your census.

TO LEARN MORE

Read more about the various people groups of early Alaskan history by visiting http://www.akhistorycourse.org/southcentral-alaska/taming-the-land-of-fire-and-ice

TIME TO REVIEW

Review Chapters 10-14 of your book before moving on to the Unit Review. See how many questions you can answer without looking at your book.

Alaska Purchase
Word Scramble Key

1.	aribkad	bidarka	A boat covered in animal skins used by Alaska Natives
2.	rtotrreyi	territory	An area of land under the authority of a ruler or state
3.	secuns	census	The process of acquiring data about the members of a specific population
4.	relwlagn	wrangell	Third-oldest community in Alaska
5.	hngirre	herring	A silvery fish that was of great commercial importance as a food fish in Alaska during the 1880s
6.	irhnsaiot	historian	People said Alaska's first census-taker was an able one of these – an expert in past events
7.	scosrcar	carcross	Bishop Bompas lived the later years of his life in this settlement
8.	ucsryv	scurvy	Many early residents in Alaska suffered from this disease caused by a deficiency of vitamin C
9.	stnlratea	translate	Turn one language into another
10.	dilteca	dialect	A particular form of a language that is peculiar to a specific region or social group

UNIT 3: ALASKA BECOMES U.S. POSSESSION

REVIEW LESSONS 10-14

Write down what you remember about:

William H. Seward – *U.S. Secretary of State who negotiated with Russia for the purchase of Alaska*

Edouard de Stoecki – *Russian ambassador who negotiated with Seward to sell Alaska to America*

Sitka – *The town in Southeast Alaska where the Russian governor of Alaska formally transferred ownership of Alaska to the United States*

Czar Alexander II – *Russian leader who sent the Russian fleet to America in 1863*

American Civil War – *A civil war fought from 1861-1865 between the Union and the Confederate (southern states that seceded in order to prevent President Abraham Lincoln from outlawing slavery in their states)*

Census – *The process of acquiring data about the members of a specific population*

Russian Orthodox Church – *Religious denomination of the Russians that settled in Alaska*

Fort Yukon – *A trading post established by Alexander Murray*

William Carpenter Bompas – *English missionary and teacher in the Yukon*

Miner – *A person who extracts ore, coal or other minerals from the earth*

George Washington Carmack – *One of the men who discovered gold along Rabbit Creek, later named Bonanza, that started the Klondike Gold Rush*

Ivan Petroff – *Alaska's first census taker*

Territory – *An area of land under the authority of a ruler or state*

Bidarka – *A boat covered in animal skins used by Native people of Alaska*

Fill in the blanks:

1) U.S. Secretary of State *William H. Seward* saw the *value* of Alaska long before the United States purchased it in *1867*.

2) With the *Civil* War raging during the early *1860*s, the United States didn't pursue purchase of Alaska until *March 1867* when Seward received word that the *Russians* were ready to unload the northern property.

3) Many Americans, including legislators, didn't think that the purchase of Alaska was a good idea because *many Americans had very little information about Alaska. They believed that it was barren and worthless. Some believed the only products in Alaska were "icebergs and polar bears."*

4) The amount of the check issued to *Russia* for the purchase of Alaska was *$7.2 million*. But some people think the check included payment for favors to help the *Union* during the American *Civil War.*

5) *Czar Alexander II* sent the Russian fleet to America in a strategic move during the year *1863*.

6) Americans eager to engage in *trade* and *commerce* flocked to Alaska before the ink was dry on the ratified treaty to purchase Russia's northern colony.

7) Alaska's *commercial herring* industry began in 1878 when 30,000 pounds were caught and preserved with salt in wooden barrels. By the turn of the century, *commercial fishing* was the leading industry as the *fur* industry declined.

8) After arriving in Unalaska in 1824, Father *Ivan Veniaminov* helped spread the *Russian Orthodox* doctrine in the Aleutians. He taught Natives in their *dialect,* Aleutian Fox, after creating an *alphabet* and translating textbooks and parts of the Bible.

9) It took *William Carpenter Bompas* more than five years to travel by ship, canoe, on foot and by dog sled from *London* to the *Yukon*, where at last he was called to become Bishop of the Yukon.

10) With no roads and only a few Native trails, Alaska's first <u>census</u> taker, <u>Ivan Petroff,</u> traveled around some parts of the territory in skin boats called <u>bidarkas</u>. His count totaled 33,426 people, including people from the following groups: <u>Caucasians, Creoles, Inuit, Aleut, Tinneh, Tlingets and Haidas.</u>

Getting an accurate count of people who lived in Alaska after it became part of the United States was challenging. And most Alaska Native people did not know that the Russians had been paid for land that their ancestors had lived on for thousands of years.

People in 1880 Alaska Census

Word Search Key

Please find the words below

Caucasian
Creole
Inuit
Aleut
Tinneh
Tlinget
Haida
Miner

Merchant
Squatter
Trapper
Trader
Fisherman
Cannery worker
Soldier
trapper

UNIT 3: ALASKA BECOMES U.S. POSSESSION

UNIT TEST

Choose *two* of the following questions to answer in paragraph form. Use as much detail as possible to completely answer the question.

1) Describe the United States purchase of Alaska. Who saw the value in Alaska and why? How much did America pay for Alaska? When was the transfer finalized?

2) What controversy surrounded the Russian fleet coming to America in 1863? Who sent the fleet? Who was happy to see the fleet arrive in New York and why?

3) Who was the Bishop of the Yukon? How did he start his mission to the Yukon? What did he do for the Native people in this region?

4) What significant information did we learn from the 1880 Alaska census? Who was the census taker? What obstacles did he face while taking the census?

TEACHER NOTES ABOUT THIS UNIT

UNIT 4: ALASKA'S FIRST GOLD RUSH

LESSON 15: GOLD FOUND IN SOUTHEAST

FACTS TO KNOW:

Prospector – A miner who searches for minerals such as gold, ore and coal
Chief Kowee – The Auk Indian chief who led Joseph Juneau and Richard Harris to gold around Juneau in 1880
Juneau – The first town to be founded in Alaska after it was purchased by the United States
Treadwell Glory Hole – One of the largest quartz lode mines in the world

COMPREHENSION QUESTIONS

1) What major find in Southeast Alaska led thousands of prospectors to the area in 1880? Who made the discovery and in what specific area?
Auk Chief Kowee, who lived on Admiralty Island, found gold nuggets in the Silver Bow Basin area of Southeast Alaska in July 1880. He brought the gold to George Pilz in Sitka in exchange for a reward. He would then take prospectors Richard Harris and Joe Juneau to locate the source of the ore. (Page 116)

2) After this major discovery, Richard Tighe Harris and Joe Juneau established the mining town of <u>Harrisburgh, later named Juneau</u>. How did the dynamics of the area change as a more white prospectors entered the area?
Trading posts, breweries and saloons popped up overnight, and by March 1881, monthly steamship service was bringing supplies to the placer miners along Gastineau Channel. (Page 118)

3) What purchase did John Treadwell make for $400 from Pierre Joseph "French Pete" Erussard? What amazing discovery did this purchase lead to?
John Treadwell bought Erussard's claim on Douglas Island. This led to the discovery of the famed Glory Hole. (Page 119)

4) What company bought out John Treadwell and his investors? When did the purchase occur? What was included in the purchase?
In 1889, the Alaska Treadwell Gold Mining Company bought out John Treadwell and his investors for $4 million. The Treadwell organization included four mines. (Page 121)

DISCUSSION QUESTION

(Discuss this question with your teacher or write your answer in essay form below. Use additional paper if necessary.)

In what ways did the early discovery of gold change Alaska's history? Consider the impact this had on Alaska's population, economy, geography, environment, etc.

_____
_____
_____
_____
_____
_____
_____
_____
_____
_____
_____
_____
_____
_____
_____
_____
_____
_____
_____
_____

ENRICHMENT ACTIVITY

Imagine that you are a journalist covering the discovery of the Treadwell Glory Hole for the local newspaper. Write your story using facts from the chapter and your imagination.

TO LEARN MORE

Read more about the early gold discoveries in Alaska by visiting http://www.akhistory-course.org/americas-territory/gold

This photograph shows 10 miners working deep inside the Treadwell Ready Bullion mine at the 1,500-foot level in 1908.

The Treadwell operation, which consisted of four mines, was the largest hard rock gold mine in the world, employing more than 2,000 people in Juneau and on Douglas Island in Southeast Alaska. Between 1881 and 1922, more than 3 million troy ounces of gold were extracted (1 troy ounce, which has its origin in the Roman monetary system and is used to weigh precious metals, is about 1.0971 ounces).

The price of gold in 1900 was a stable $20.67 per ounce, which is about $525 in 2017.

UNIT 4: ALASKA'S FIRST GOLD RUSH

LESSON 16: EXPLORING THE NILE OF ALASKA

FACTS TO KNOW:

Lt. Frederick Schwatka – He was commissioned by the U.S. Army to explore the Yukon River

Yukon River – A large river (more than 2,000 miles long) that stretches from Alaska to Canada

Barka – A small-decked boat

COMPREHENSION QUESTIONS

1) Why was Lt. Frederick Schwatka commissioned by the U.S. Army to explore the "Nile of Alaska"? What is the actual name of this river?
Lt. Frederick Schwatka was commissioned by the U.S. Army to find out more about the Yukon River and the Native people of that region. (Page 123)

2) Describe Lt. Schwatca's journey. Who did he travel with? How did he travel?
In the summer of 1883, Lt. Frederick Schwatka traversed the upper Yukon River by raft from the lakes at its source to Fort Selkirk. Schwatka traveled with Dr. Wilson, topographical assistant Homan, Sgt. Gloster, Cpl. Shircliff, Pvt. Roth and Mr. McIntosh, as well as a myriad of Indian guides. (Page 124)

3) Name three things that Lt. Frederick learned about this region and/or its people.
He came upon two lakes that he named Lindemann and Bennett. He learned about the flora and fauna abundant in the area. He learned about the smoke signals that the Chilkats and Tagish used to communicate that announced they were ready to trade. (Pages 124-125)

4) How long did it take Lt. Schwatka to complete his trip? How did his trip end?
It took Lt. Schwatka about three months to float the almost 2,000 miles to the delta, although his raft journey of almost more than 1,300 miles came to an end at the trading station of Nuklakayet. His party loaded a barka and drifted a little until they met a trading steamer that took the barka in tow. (Page 126)

DISCUSSION QUESTION

(Discuss this question with your teacher or write your answer in essay form below. Use additional paper if necessary.)

What complaint did Lt. Frederick Schwatka have about the British map after his time on the "Nile of Alaska?"

_____
_____
_____
_____
_____
_____
_____
_____
_____
_____
_____
_____
_____
_____
_____
_____
_____

TO LEARN MORE

To learn more about the Yukon River, look for these books at your local library:
Lifeline to the Yukon – A History of Yukon River Navigation. By Anderson, Barry C. Seattle: Superior Publishing Company, 1983.

Yukon River Steamboats-A Pictorial History. By Cohen, Stan. Missoula, Montana: Pictorial Histories Publishing Company, 1982.

MAP ACTIVITY

Trace the Yukon River on this map. Mark where it begins and ends.

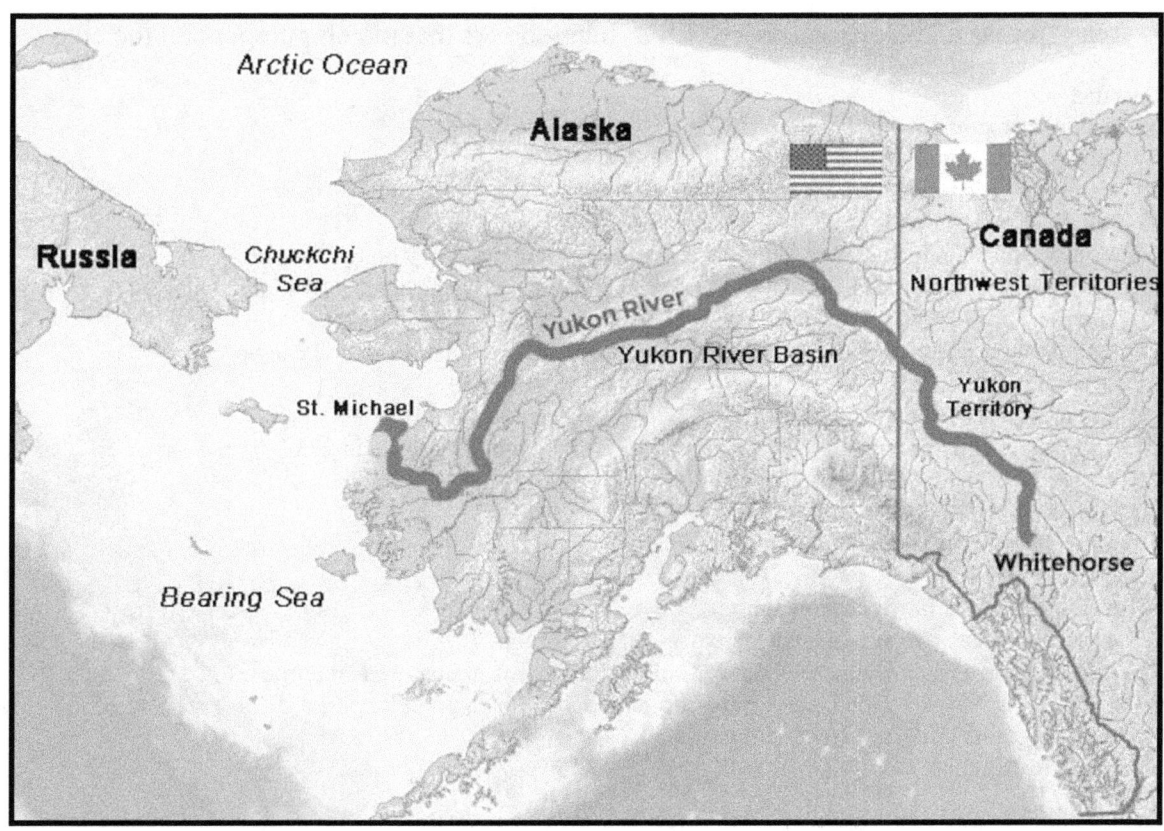

First Gold Rush and Exploration
Crossword Puzzle

Read Across and Down clues and fill in blank boxes that match numbers on the clues

Across

4   The highest point of a hill or mountain
7   Closely compacted together, crowded
10 A ship that is propelled by a steam engine
12 Tall, fast-growing trees of north temperate regions
16 A piece of land almost surrounded by water or projecting out into a body of water
18 A hollow or depression in the earth's surface, wholly or partly surrounded by higher land
19 The fixed portion of food or other goods allowed to each person
20 A naturally occurring solid material from which a metal or valuable mineral can be profitably extracted
22 The precious yellow metal that brought many people to Alaska
24 A town named after one of the discoverers of gold in Southeast Alaska in 1880
25 People who search for mineral deposits
30 Longest river in Alaska
31 A length of water wider than a strait, joining two larger areas of water
32 A long, narrow, typically vertical hole that gives access to a mine
33 A sailing ship with two or more masts
35 A place between two mountains where one can go through
36 An important assignment carried out for political, religious or commercial purposes
37 A journey or voyage undertaken by a group of people with a particular purpose
38 Especially fine or decorative clothing
39 Small-decked boat

Down

1   The act of raising or lifting something
2   A small, solid lump of gold
3   Auk chief who took miners Juneau and Harris to Southeast Alaska gold deposit in 1880
5   An island across from Juneau where the Treadwell Mine was established
6   A mineral in the form of a hard, shiny crystal
8   A step like part of a mine where minerals are being extracted
9   The animals of a particular region, habitat or geological period
11 A tributary stream of a river close to or forming part of its source
13 One of the first names for the town of Juneau
14 A river or stream flowing into a larger river or lake
15 A course, way or road for passage or travel
17 A name associated with a group of people rushing to Alaska to search for gold
21 The action of finding something, like Joe Juneau and gold in Silver Bow Basin
22 A narrow and steep-sided ravine marking the course of a fast stream
23 Place where the largest amount of gold, silver, etc., in a particular area can be found
26 Extremely large or great

First Gold Rush and Exploration
Crossword Puzzle Key

Down (Continued)
27 An amount of material, provisions or money supplied to a prospector to search for ore in return for a share in the resulting profits
28 Travel across or through
29 An alluvial, marine or glacial deposit containing particles of valuable mineral
34 The plants of a particular region, habitat or geological period

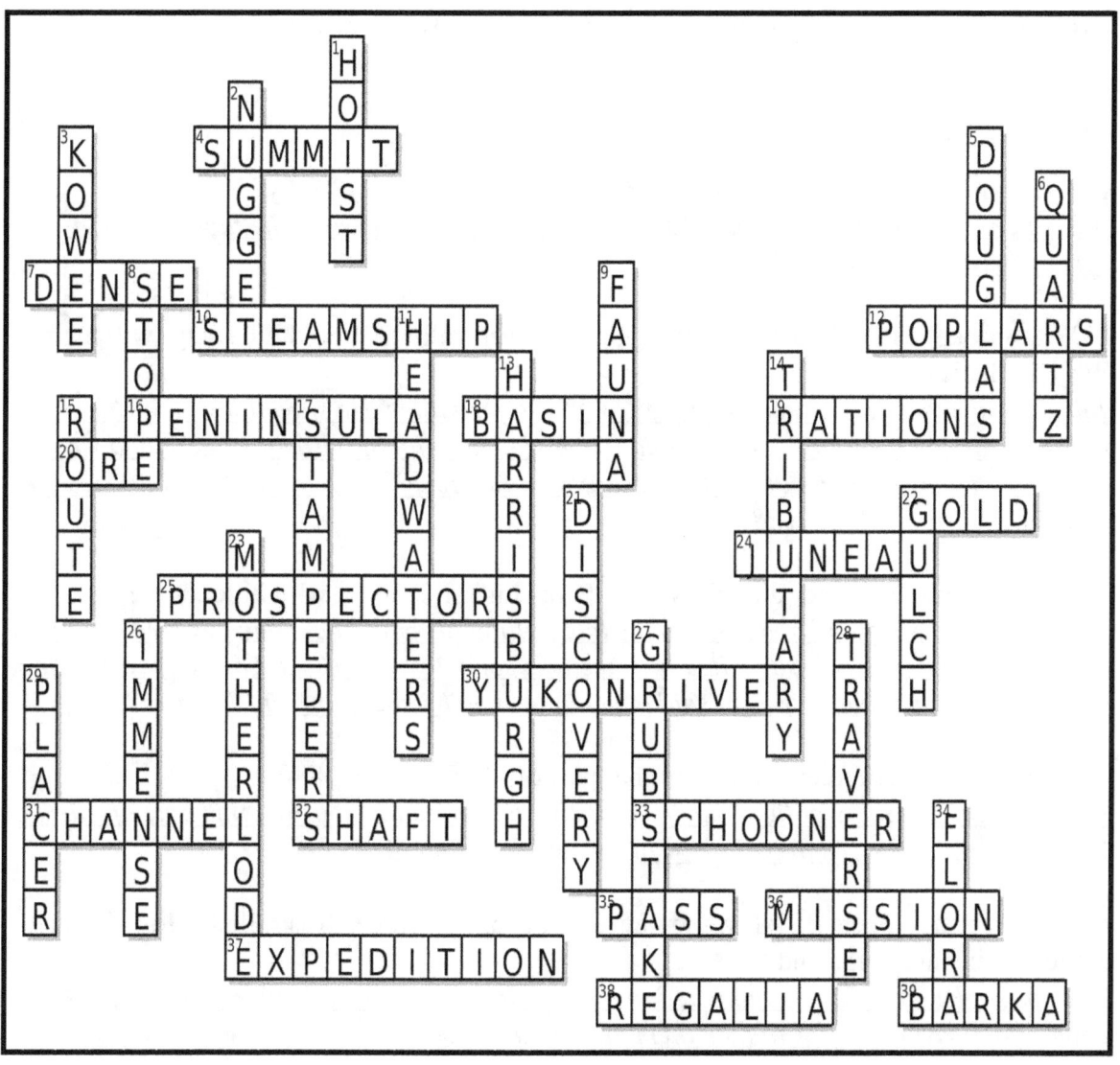

UNIT 4: ALASKA'S FIRST GOLD RUSH

LESSON 17: OLD JOHN BREMNER

FACTS TO KNOW:

John Bremner – A Scotsman who came to Alaska to look for gold and was mysteriously killed
Whipsaw – A two-man saw used to cut down trees
John Minook – The man who brought word back to Nukukyet that John Bremner had been killed
Rampart – Once an important trading post and supply center for thousands of miners

COMPREHENSION QUESTIONS

1) What three bodies of water were named after John Bremner? Why?
Bremener River, John River and Old John Lake all bear witness to the fact that John Bremner was there. (Page 128)

2) What brought John Bremner to the Copper River Valley? Who did he stay with there? Why did he leave?
John Bremner was a prospector in the Copper River Valley. He stayed with the Copper Indians – or "Ma Nuskas" as he called them. He had a lot of hardships there and was easily persuaded to go on an exploring trip with Lt. Henry Allen to the Tanana, Koyukuk and Yukon rivers. (Pages 128-129)

3) How did John Bremner die? Why was there confusion about who killed him?
John Bremner was killed at a fish camp while putting his boat back in the water. There was confusion about who actually killed him because some informants said one of two men had shot Bremner, but another report said a medicine man finished him off. (Page 131)

4) What was law enforcement like in that part of Alaska in the 1880s?
Law, as represented by police, sheriffs and courts, had not penetrated this part of Alaska in the 1880s. There was only the law of the miners. (Page 132)

5) What did the miners do when they heard that John Bremner was killed? How did they settle the dispute in the end?
The miners held a meeting and voted to avenge John Bremner's death. They forced the captain of a river steamer to take them up the Koyukuk to where John was killed. They

captured two men that tried to escape. One young man confessed, but some of the miners thought that he only confessed out of fear of the other man, who was a shaman. After a vote, they hung the young man and let the shaman go. (Pages 132-136)

6) What was the name of the first boat to go up the Koyukuk River? *The Explorer.* (Page 135)

DISCUSSION QUESTION

(Discuss this question with your teacher or write your answer in essay form below. Use additional paper if necessary.)

How do you think the case of John Bremner's death might have been different if there was official law enforcement in Koyukuk county at the time of his murder?

_____
_____
_____
_____
_____
_____
_____
_____
_____
_____
_____
_____
_____
_____
_____
_____
_____
_____

ENRICHMENT ACTIVITY

Imagine that you are a prospector in Southeast Alaska in the 1880s. Write a journal entry about one of your adventures. Where did you go? Who did you meet? Were you successful?

TO LEARN MORE

Read more about mining in Alaska by visiting http://www.akhistorycourse.org/americas-territory/alaskas-heritage/chapter-4-15-mining

UNIT 4: ALASKA'S FIRST GOLD RUSH

LESSON 18: RICH NAMES ALONG THE KOYUKUK

FACTS TO KNOW:

Gordon Bettles – Pioneer of the Koyukuk country who set up several "bean shops" (trading posts)

Stampeders – The men and women who rushed to Alaska to search for gold

Revenue Cutter – Steamers that enforced custom and navigation laws under the U.S. Revenue Service, upon which the U.S. Coast Guard later was modeled

COMPREHENSION QUESTIONS

1) What evidence was there that prospectors were looking for gold along the Koyukuk river before the Klondike Gold Rush?
Evidence that people were there before the Klondike Gold Rush include rusty fragments of mining tools, unmistakable disturbance of the surface and a weathered ax mark on a tree. (Page 140)

2) What are some of the unique features of the Koyukuk as described by Lt. B.H. Camden who traveled there?
One of the most noticeable features of the Koyukuk was in the formation of its bars, which were composed of gravel, not sand as along the Yukon. Also Mastodon Bank, a glacial formation that seemed to be the graveyard of mastodons for many teeth and bones belonging to that animal were found there. (Page 142)

3) The first streams on the Koyukuk to yield gold in large quantities were *Myrtle*, *Emma* and *Gold* creeks, and as early as 1899, the town of *Slate* Creek was started.

4) Name three of the places in the Koyukuk region named for prospectors.
Some of the places named for prospectors in the Koyukuk region are Wiseman Creek, Bettles, Bergman and Hughes City. (Pages 138-143)

5) Why did mining in the Koyukuk region become less important after the second boom in 1915?
By 1916, the richest claims of both Nolan Creek and Hammond River were mined, and the high wages of World War I convinced many of the most energetic men to leave. Its heyday was over, and mining was never so important again in this area. (Page 147)

DISCUSSION QUESTIONS

(Discuss this question with your teacher or write your answer in essay form below. Use additional paper if necessary.)

Who was the Blueberry Kid? Summarize his mysterious story.

_____
_____
_____
_____
_____
_____
_____
_____
_____
_____
_____
_____
_____
_____
_____
_____
_____
_____
_____
_____

ENRICHMENT ACTIVITY

Learn more about what life was like for a miner during the gold rush by downloading and reading *The Rush for Gold* comic book. Read it online by visiting http://www.akhistory-course.org/comic/AK_Economy_pp56-109.pdf

TO LEARN MORE

Look for this book at your local library to learn more about the people of the Koyukuk region: *Up the Koyukuk.* Alaska Geographic, 1 0:4 (1983).

TIME TO REVIEW

Review Chapters 15-18 of your book before moving on to the Unit Review. See how many questions you can answer without looking at your book.

Rich Names Along the Koyukuk
Word Search Puzzle Key

Words

- Koyukuk
- Batzna
- Moses Village
- Allakaket
- Nok
- Kakliaklia
- Wiseman
- Hughes
- Bettles
- Coldfoot
- Interior
- Evans Bar
- Yukon
- Mastodon Bank
- Slate Creek

UNIT 4: ALASKA'S FIRST GOLD RUSH

REVIEW LESSONS 15-18

What do you remember about:

Prospectors – *A miner who searches for minerals such as gold, ore and coal*

Chief Kowee – *Auk Indian chief who led Joseph Juneau and Richard Harris to gold around Juneau in 1880*

Juneau – *The first town to be founded in Alaska after it was purchased by the United States*

Treadwell Glory Hole – *One of the largest quartz lode mines in the world*

Lt. Frederick Schwatka – *He was commissioned by the U.S. Army to the Nile of Alaska*

Yukon River – *Large river (over 2,000 miles long) stretching from Alaska to Canada*

Barka – *A small-decked boat*

John Bremner – *A Scotsman who came to Alaska to look for gold and was mysteriously killed*

Whipsaw – *A two-man saw used to cut down trees*

John Minook – *The man who brought word back to Nukukyet that John Bremner had been killed*

Rampart – *Once an important trading post and supply center for thousands of miners*

Gordon Bettles – *Pioneer of the Koyukuk country who set up several "bean shops" (trading posts)*

Stampeders – *The men and women who rushed to Alaska to search for gold*

Revenue Cutter – *Steamer that enforced custom and navigation laws under the U.S. Revenue Service, upon which the U.S. Coast Guard later was modeled*

Fill in the blanks:

1) Chief _Kowee_ led _Joseph Juneau_ and _Richard Harris_ to gold near what became the town of _Juneau_ in 1880.

2) The influx of white _prospectors_ changed the dynamics of the area. _Trading posts_, _breweries_ and _saloons_ popped up overnight, and by March 1881, monthly _steamship_ service was bringing supplies to the placer miners along Gaustineau Channel.

3) In 1889, _Alaska Treadwell Gold Mining_ Company bought out _John Treadwell_ and his investors for $4 million. The _Alaska Treadwell Gold Mining_ organization included four mines and the famed _Treadwell Glory_ Hole.

4) In the summer of 1883, _Lt. Frederick Schwatka_ traversed the upper _Yukon_ River by raft in order to gather information about _the Indian tribes in the region, as well as study geographical details._

5) _Lt. Frederick Schwatka_'s exploration of the _Yukon_ River gave the world a firsthand account of the river and the lay of the land. Three things that he learned were: _He came upon two lakes that he named Lindemann and Bennett. He learned about the flora and fauna abundant in the area. He learned about the smoke signals that the Chilkats and Tagish used to communicate that they were ready to trade._

6) _John Bremner_ lived a life of hardship among the _Copper_ Indians in 1880. He was killed at a _fish_ camp along the _Koyukuk_ River while putting his boat back in the water.

7) A man named _John Minook_, part Russian and part Native, brought news of the murder of _John Bremner_ to about 60 prospectors. The prospectors decided to avenge his death and _hijacked_ the little river steamer named _Explorer_ in order to get back to the scene of the crime.

8) Long before the Klondike Gold Rush, evidence of _prospectors_ plying the waters of the _Koyukuk_ River were found such as: _the rusty fragments of iron implements and weathered ax marks on trees._

9) Three people, *Fiddler John, Dutch Marie* and *Frank Adams* disappeared from Bettles in *1912* after they boarded the *The Blueberry Kid*'s launch.

10) *The Blueberry Kid* alone reached Nulato and took a steamboat to St. Michael. It is said that he cashed out thousands of dollars of *gold dust* at the Mint, and again in San Francisco.

Old John Bremner
Word Scramble Puzzle Key

Please unscramble the words below

1.	zliezrdg	grizzled	Having or streaked with gray hair
2.	jonualr	journal	A daily record of news and events of a personal nature, similar to a diary
3.	pwshwia	whipsaw	A saw with a narrow blade and a handle at both ends, used typically by two people
4.	grub	grub	Food
5.	nveaeg	avenge	To punish someone who has harmed you or someone or something that you care about
6.	erdmiskba	disembark	To leave a ship or boat
7.	nreeteiprrt	interpreter	A person to translates from one language to another
8.	neemrbr	bremner	Man for whom the John River is named
9.	hccae	cache	Food and supplies are kept away from animals in this place
10.	inpapotira	apparition	A supernatural appearance of a person or thing

UNIT 4: ALASKA'S FIRST GOLD RUSH

UNIT TEST

Choose *two* of the following questions to answer in paragraph form. Use as much detail as possible to completely answer the question.

1) Describe the impact of Alaska's first gold rush. Consider how it changed Alaska's population, economy, geography, etc.

2) Who was commissioned by the U.S. Army to travel the upper Yukon River in 1880? How did he travel up the river? What was the purpose of his trip? What did he learn about the area and its people?

3) Summarize one of the two murder mysteries that happened in the Koyukuk River region. What happened? Who was involved in the story? How did it end?

4) What were some of the features of the Koyukuk River around 1900? What do you know about some of the people of that region?

TEACHER NOTES ABOUT THIS UNIT

UNIT 5: DREAMS OF GOLD

LESSON 19: ALASKA'S SECOND GOLD RUSH

FACTS TO KNOW:

Peter Doroshin – Mining engineer who explored the Kenai Peninsula in 1849
Grubstake – Usually consisted of enough food and supplies to keep a man for one season
Kenai Peninsula – A large peninsula on the southern coast of Alaska
Hydraulic mining – Use of a high-pressure water jet to break up gravel and make mining more efficient

COMPREHENSION QUESTIONS

1) What was the only recorded official gold-hunting expedition that was made by the Russian-American Company? Who was the prospector? What area did he explore?
In 1849, the Russian-America Company sent mining engineer Peter Doroschin to the Kenai area to search for gold. (Pages 148)

2) Why do historians speculate that the Russians did not announce their findings of gold in the Cook Inlet area?
Some historians speculate that the Russian government knew there were gold deposits in Alaska, but it didn't broadcast the fact because it feared a rush of gold-seeking Americans or British into its colonies. (Page 150)

3) Describe Alexander King's prospecting trip to the Kenai Peninsula in 1880. What deal did he arrange with Capt. Charles Swanson? What important discovery did he make? Why was this discovery significant?
Around 1888, a prospector named Alexander King arrived at Kenai and convinced Capt. Charles Swanson, who owned a trading post, to grubstake him for two summers and a winter. King rowed up the Turnagain Arm. He returned the second summer with four pokes of gold and paid off his grubstake. Five years later his discoveries at Resurrection Creek, Mills Creek and Sixmile Creek drew streams of prospectors to the area. (Pages 150-151)

4) By the year *1896*, Alaska's *second* gold rush was in full swing. Articles in large newspapers like the The *San Francisco Chronicle* and *The New York Times* drew about 3,000 prospectors to *Cook Inlet.* (Page 152)

5) Why was the Cook Inlet gold rush short-lived? How did it end?
The Cook Inlet rush ended about as abruptly as it started. By the spring of 1897, hundreds of people had left the area. The best sites had already been claimed. Although another rush of people poured into the area in 1898, most left after efficient hydraulic mining equipment arrived that drove out the small prospectors. (Page 154)

6) Why was Alexander King hung on October 2, 1900?
King confessed to killing a man named Herbert Davenport while working on a freighter in 1900. He was hung by the Royal Canadian Mounted Police. (Page 155)

DISCUSSION QUESTION

(Discuss this question with your teacher or write your answer in essay form below. Use additional paper if necessary.)

What have you learned about the mining process? Was it simple or complicated? Explain your answer.

_____
_____
_____
_____
_____
_____
_____
_____
_____
_____
_____
_____

ENRICHMENT ACTIVITY

Imagine that you want to hire a miner to find gold for you in Alaska in 1900. Write a "Help Wanted" classified ad that includes the qualities that you are looking for in a miner and what tools you require the miner to own. Consider what you have learned about successful miners so far in this course.

TO LEARN MORE

Read more about the early mining in Alaska's interior by visiting: http://www.akhistory-course.org/interior-alaska/1869-1896-stars-and-stripes-up-the-river

UNIT 5: DREAMS OF GOLD

LESSON 20: DREAMS OF SALMON TURN TO GOLD

FACTS TO KNOW:

George Washington Carmack – He was credited with starting the Klondike Gold Rush

Tagish Charley (Dawson Charlie) Mason – Codiscoverer of gold at Rabbit Creek that started the Klondike Gold Rush

Skookum Jim Mason – Codiscoverer of gold at Rabbit Creek that started the Klondike Gold Rush

Discovery Claim – The first claim in a region and center point of a mining district

COMPREHENSION QUESTIONS

1) Unlike most hard-working prospectors, George Washington Carmack had time for the finer things in life. Like what?
In his cabin he had an organ and a library, including such journals as Scientific American and Review of Reviews. He enjoyed talking on scientific matters and writing sentimental poetry like his, "Christmas Thoughts." (Page 158)

2) George Washington Carmack had a premonition while sitting in the ruins of old Fort Selkirk in 1896. What was his premonition? What did he do after he had the premonition? How did that premonition lead him to the Throndiuk (later called Klondike).
He had a premonition that a great change was coming into his life. He flipped a coin to see if he should go upstream or downstream to Fortymile. That night, he had a dream about fish covered with gold nuggets and $20 gold pieces for eyes. He took this as a sign to go fishing at the Throndiuk. This fishing trip eventually led him and his companions to find gold at the Klondike. (Pages 159-161)

3) Why is August 17, 1896 a memorable day that is still celebrated in Yukon Territory? What happened on this day?
While waiting for his friends to join him, Skookum Jim looked at the sand of the creek where he'd gone to get a drink. He found gold, he said, in greater quantities than he had ever seen before. That was August 17, 1896. This discovery began the Klondike Gold Rush. (Page 163)

4) Explain the dispute between George Washington Carmack, Tagish Charley and Skookum Jim about the discovery claim. What did they eventually agree upon and why?
Skookum Jim thought the Discovery Claim on Rabbit Creek should be his by right of discovery, but Carmack told him that an Indian would not be allowed to record it. They finally decided the question by Carmack staking the Discovery Claim and assigning a half interest in it to Jim. (Page 164)

5) What did George Washington Carmack do on the way to the mining recorder's office that sent a rush of prospectors to the Klondike?
Carmack first stopped off at Bill McPhee's saloon on his way to the mining recorder's office. He announced at the bar that he had found gold in the Klondike region and showed off some of what he found. By midnight, a stampede was in full swing. (Page 165)

6) Why did George Washington Carmack eventually leave his wife, Kate, and end his partnerships with Tagish Charley and Skookum Jim?
Carmack eventually dissolved his partnerships with Charley and Jim and left Kate because he could not tolerate their drinking alcohol any longer. (Page 169)

7) How did the discovery of gold in the Klondike in 1896 help the United States out of a deep depression?
The Klondike gold loosened up capital all over the world, stimulated inventiveness and gave employment to many. It helped San Francisco, revived Portland, Oregon, and was the making of Seattle. It was the last of the great international gold rushes. (Page 172)

DISCUSSION QUESTION

(Discuss this question with your teacher or write your answer in essay form below. Use additional paper if necessary.)

In what ways do you think the Klondike gold rush changed Alaska's economy and population?

_____
_____
_____
_____
_____
_____
_____
_____
_____
_____

ENRICHMENT ACTIVITY

Chapter 20 began with a poem written by George Washington Carmack. Find another poem written by a famous person in Alaska's history. See if you can discover what happened in the poet's life to cause him or her to write that particular poem. Use books and online resources to do your research.

TO LEARN MORE

Read about what happened to the *S.S. Portland* by visiting http://www.akhistorycourse.org/americas-territory/wreck-of-the-ss-portland-found

Prospecting in the Klondike was tough work.

UNIT 5: DREAMS OF GOLD

LESSON 21: LUCKIEST MAN ON THE KLONDIKE

FACTS TO KNOW:

Clarence Berry – "The luckiest man on the Klondike" who strikes it rich after hearing of George Washington Carmack's discovery
Throndiuk – Indian word for Klondike
Bonanza Creek – Rabbit Creek was later renamed Bonanza Creek after gold was discovered there
S.S. Portland – One of two steamships filled with gold and miners from the Klondike
S.S. Excelsior – One of two steamships filled with gold and miners from the Klondike

COMPREHENSION QUESTIONS

1) How did Clarence Berry begin his prospecting journey? What obstacles did he face?
Before Clarence Berry struck gold, he did not have enough money to pay his rent. He borrowed somewhere between $40-$60 to finance his trip. He was one of the few that was able to get through the storms to Fortymile. He didn't find riches at first, but he found work at $100 a day and secured a claim. (Pages 173-174)

2) Who was the "Bride of the Klondike"? What advice did she give to other women travelers to Alaska?
Ethel was Clarence's wife who traveled with him to the mining camp. Her advice to women was to stay away from Alaska because it was no place for a woman go alone. She said it was much better for a man if he has a wife with him to cook for him and help him. (Pages 174-175)

3) How did George Washington Carmack's announcement at Bill McPhee's Bar change Clarence Berry's fortune?
Clarence Berry was bartending the day that George Washington Carmack came rushing in to tell of striking it rich on the Klondike. He then led stampeders from the Alaska side of the line over the upriver trail to Carmack's Klondike and staked his claim. (Page 176)

4) Describe the process that Clarence Berry and his partner, Anton Stander, used to mine in the winter.
Night after night they burned frozen ground; day after day, they shoveled up what they had thawed. (Page 177)

5) How did the Berrys travel back to California? What did they bring back with them? What did they tell reporters about the Klondike?
The Berrys took one of two little steamers filled with other successful prospectors to St. Michael, where they boarded the Excelsior bound for San Francisco. Friends helped them drag a sagging suitcase and two wooden boxes filled with gold aboard. They told reporters, "The Klondike is the richest gold field in the world." (Pages 179-180)

6) How did Clarence Berry repay Bill McPhee? What did he repay him for?
Bill McPhee, Clarence Berry's boss at the bar, grubstaked him for the stampede to the Klondike. In 1906, fire destroyed McPhee's saloon, and well along in years, McPhee lost everything but the clothes he was wearing. Berry offered to pay whatever was need to rebuild his business and later provided a pension for McPhee. (Page 182)

DISCUSSION QUESTION

(Discuss this question with your teacher or write your answer in essay form below. Use additional paper if necessary.)

What was the difference between how Clarence Berry and George Washington Carmack handled their new-found wealth?

_____
_____
_____
_____
_____
_____
_____
_____
_____
_____

TO LEARN MORE

To read more about the Klondike Gold Rush, look for this book at your local library: *One Man's Gold Rush: A Klondike Album.* Seattle: University of Washington Press and Vancouver: Douglas and McIntyre, 1967.

TIME TO REVIEW

Review Chapters 19-21 of your book before moving on to the Unit Review. See how many questions you can answer without looking at your book.

UNIT 5: DREAMS OF GOLD

REVIEW LESSONS 19-21

What do you remember about:

Peter Doroshin – *Mining engineer who explored the Kenai Peninsula in 1849*

Grubstake – *Usually consisted of enough food and supplies to keep a man for one season*

Kenai Peninsula – *A large peninsula on the southern coast of Alaska*

Hydraulic mining – *Use of a high-pressure water jet to break up gravel and make mining more efficient*

George Washington Carmack – *He was credited with starting the Klondike Gold Rush*

Tagish Charley (Dawson Charlie) Mason – *Codiscoverer of gold at Rabbit Creek that started the Klondike Gold Rush*

Skookum Jim Mason – *Codiscoverer of gold at Rabbit Creek that started the Klondike Gold Rush*

Discovery Claim – *The first claim in a region and center point of a mining district*

Clarence Berry – *"The luckiest man on the Klondike," strikes it rich after hearing of George Washington Carmack's discovery*

Throndiuk – *Indian word for Klondike*

Bonanza Creek – *Rabbit Creek was later renamed Bonanza Creek after gold was discovered there*

S.S. Portland – *One of two steamships filled with gold and miners from the Klondike*

S.S. Excelsior – *One of two steamships filled with gold and miners from the Klondike*

Fill in the blanks:

1) In the year *1849*, the Russian-American Company sent mining engineer *Peter Doroshin* to the *Kenai* area to search for gold.

2) Around 1888, a prospector named *Alexander King* arrived at *Kenai* and convinced Capt. Charles Swanson, who owned a trading post, to *grubstake* him for two summers and a winter.

3) Mining was *simple*. The liberal use of a *pick* and a *shovel*, as well as a strong back, was all that most men needed.

4) While waiting for his friends *George Washington Carmack* and T*agish Charley* to join him, Skookum Jim looked at the sand of the creek where he'd gone to get a drink. He found *gold*, he said, in greater quantities than he had ever seen before. That was on the date *August 17, 1896*, a memorable day that still is celebrated in the *Yukon* Territory.

5) *Skookum Jim* thought the *Discovery Claim* on Rabbit Creek should be his by right of discovery, but Carmack told him that an Indian would not be allowed to record it.

6) After *George Carmack, Skookum Jim* and *Tagish Charley* discovered gold along Rabbit Creek, they renamed their find "*Bonanza*" and built sluice boxes to sift out the *gold*.

7) In 1896, the United States was in the third year of a severe *depression*. The Klondike gold loosened up *capital* all over the world, stimulated inventiveness and gave *employment* to many. It was the last of the great international *gold rushes*.

8) A few years before Lady Luck showered riches on *Clarence Berry*, the "luckiest man on the *Klondike*" didn't have enough money to pay his room rent or ask his sweetheart *Ethel* to marry him.

9) To make ends meet, *Clarence Berry* took a job tending bar at *Bill McPhee's saloon*. He was bartending the day that *George Washington Carmack* came rushing in to tell of striking it rich on the *Throndiuk/Klondike or Rabbit Creek or Bonanza*.

10) When the S.S. *Excelsior* docked in *San Francisco* on July 14, 1897, the *Berrys* told reporters, "*The Klondike* is the richest gold field in the world."

11) *Clarence* and *Ethel* carried *sacks, jars and bottles filled with gold* off the steamship.

UNIT 5: DREAMS OF GOLD

UNIT TEST

Choose *two* of the following questions to answer in paragraph form. Use as much detail as possible to completely answer the question.

1) How did the Cook Inlet gold rush begin? Who made the first discovery and when? How did it end and why?

2) Compare and contrast the stories of George Washington Carmack and Clarence Berry. What similarities can you find about their journeys to the Klondike? What was different? Compare how Carmack and Berry handled their new-found wealth.

3) What did you learn about the mining process of the 1800s? What kind of tools were used? How did the process change during the winter?

4) How did the Klondike gold rush impact the United States economy in 1896? How did it impact the history of Alaska?

_____
_____
_____
_____
_____
_____
_____
_____
_____
_____
_____
_____
_____
_____
_____
_____
_____
_____
_____
_____

TEACHER NOTES ABOUT THIS UNIT

Dreams of Gold
Crossword Puzzle

Read Across and Down clues and fill in blank boxes that match numbers on the clues

Across
2   The name of the creek where George Washington Carmack and his friends found gold
6   This mining town bordered Resurrection Creek
7   This mining town grew to be the largest settlement in Cook Inlet after gold was discovered in 1896
9   A tool for breaking hard rock, with a long wooden handle and a curved metal bar
11 This ship arrived in Seattle on July 17, 1897, loaded with gold from the Klondike
16 A boat with a narrow, flat bottom, high bow and flaring sides
17 One of George Washington Carmack's friends
18 A bag miners used to carry gold
22 A person who searches for gold
23 Waste left over after gold has been processed
26 Alexander King rowed up this Arm, known for its swift tides, in 1888
27 Unchartered territory
28 George Washington Carmack had a premonition while sitting among the rocks at this location
29 This ship carried Klondike gold to San Francisco in July 1897
30 A place of excavating, especially for gold
31 One of George Washington Carmack's friends
32 A risky or daring journey or undertaking
33 A strong feeling that something is about to happen

Down
1   A long arduous journey, typically on foot
3   Rabbit Creek was renamed this after Carmack discovered gold there in 1896
4   A person newly arrived in the mining districts of Alaska
5   A small shelter made of wood and situated in a wild or remote area
8   A large flat-bottomed boat with broad square ends used to haul gold
10 Caribou Crossing was later renamed this name
11 Supplies
12 A form of mining that extracts gold from a placer deposit using a pan
13 A small piece of land near Clarence Berry's claim that was rich with gold
14 George Washington Carmack told the people at this settlement about his gold discovery
15 To wash gold by rinsing with water
19 Area of the Yukon where George Washington Carmack found a fortune in gold
20 Creek where gold was found in Cook Inlet area in 1896
21 The hard area of rock in the ground that holds up the loose soil above

Dreams of Gold
Crossword Puzzle Key

Down (Continued)
24 Port where the *Excelsior* and the *Portland* loaded up with gold and gold miners to head to Seattle and San Francisco in 1897
25 A tract of land having access to a vein or lode of gold

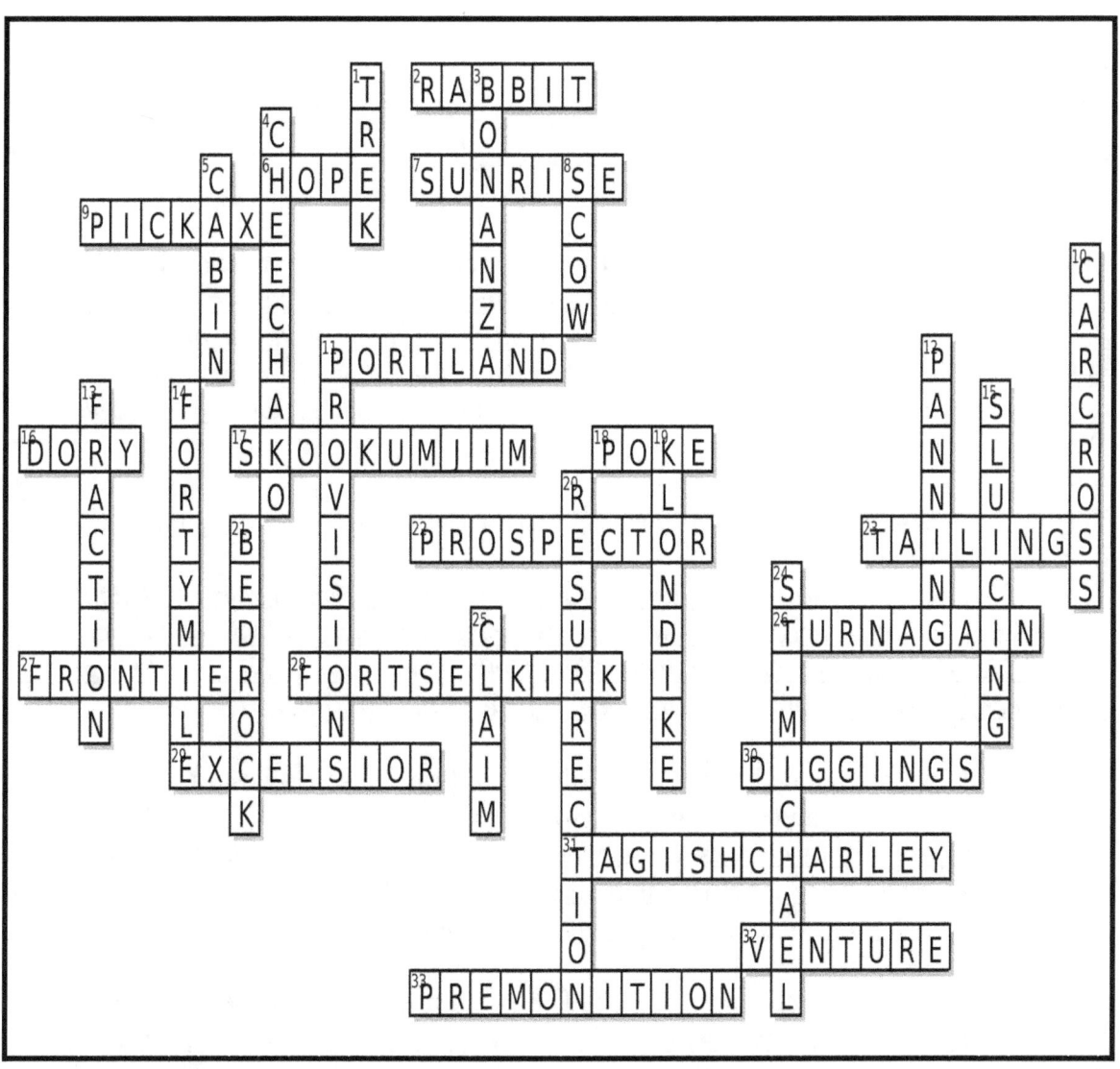

UNIT 6: RUSH TO THE KLONDIKE

LESSON 22: DAWSON IS BORN

FACTS TO KNOW:

Dawson City – A city on the Yukon that became the center of the Klondike Gold Rush
Joseph Ladue – Founder of Dawson City
Kate Ryan – Canadian nurse who traveled to Dawson City for adventure

COMPREHENSION QUESTIONS

1) Who was Dawson City named for? Why?
Dawson City was named after George M. Dawson, head of the Geological Survey of Canada who surveyed the area and noted its possibilities for gold a decade before. (Page 183)

2) What offer did Joseph Ladue make to Lt. Frederick Schwatka? What happened next?
As he was trading along the river, Joseph Ladue met Lt. Frederick Schwatka near the Alaska-Yukon border. He didn't think the raft would make it down the Yukon, and he tried to sell the lieutenant a small scow. When Schwatka turned down the offer, Ladue hopped on the explorer's raft and floated with the party another 350 miles down to Fort Yukon. (Page 184)

3) How did Joseph Ladue profit off the gold rush? How did the growing population increase his business?
Joseph Ladue owned a sawmill and supplied miners with the lumber they needed to build sluice boxes and other necessities. He sold lots on the settlement in Dawson for between $5 and $25. By late July 1897, the district had 5,000 people and Ladue raised his prices to between $800 and $8,000. Town lots later fetched $40,000. (Pages 184-185)

4) Dawson City became the largest city north of San Francisco and west of Winnipeg. What were some of the amenities that Dawson City offered?
Dawson City provided its citizens with steam heating, running water, electricity and phone service. Dawson resembled a large cosmopolitan city with dozens of hotels, motion picture theaters, a hospital and many restaurants. (Pages 186-187)

5) Why were fires a common occurrence in Dawson City? What was the fire department like? *The extreme cold, coupled with dryness, meant fires burned in all buildings when occupied. Very hot stove pipes behind flimsy walls were often the culprit. The Dawson*

volunteer fire department built a fire hall and tower down near the bank of the Yukon River by 1897. The fire department would ring a bell in the tower when there was a fire. They used a hose cart, which extended only as far as the city's water system. (Pages 192-193)

DISCUSSION QUESTION

(Discuss this question with your teacher or write your answer in essay form below. Use additional paper if necessary.)

Who was Kate Ryan? Why did she come to the Klondike? What did she do when she got there? *(Pages 198-201)*

_____
_____
_____
_____
_____
_____
_____
_____
_____
_____
_____
_____
_____
_____
_____

ENRICHMENT ACTIVITY

The gold rush provided an opportunity for people like Joseph Ladue to establish a new city. Create your own 1896 gold rush city. Draw a map of your city and label all of the important landmarks in your city. Consider what businesses, services and organizations would be important for the people of your city.

TO LEARN MORE

Look for this book at your local library:
The Klondike Fever, Pierre Berton. New York: Alfred Knopf, 1967.

UNIT 6: RUSH TO THE KLONDIKE

LESSON 23: ST. MICHAEL AWAKENS

FACTS TO KNOW:

St. Michael – Once a sleepy old Russian village, it became a hub for those coming from and going to the Yukon

Steamer – A little boat typically designed to transport a small number of people, but were often overcrowded to carry stampeders to and from St. Michael

All-water route – Route people took to the Klondike gold fields by steamship from Seattle to St. Michael and then on smaller boats on the Yukon River to Dawson

COMPREHENSION QUESTIONS

1) How did St. Michael "awaken" on June 25, 1897?
On June 25, 1897, the sleepy old Russian town of St. Michael awoke when the river steamer Alice arrived with 25 miners from Dawson carrying $500,000 among them in gold dust. St. Michael became the hub for those coming from and going to the Yukon. (Pages 202-203)

2) Explain why St. Michael was an important stop to the Yukon? How did this fact create a need in St. Michael?
Many prospectors took large steamships from Seattle to St. Michael, but they then had to find alternative means to travel the Yukon River to Dawson. Large steamships were prohibited from entering into the deep current that was covered in debris. All passengers and cargo had to land at St. Michael and transfer to small steamers. The demand for small steamships to carry passengers to the Klondike exploded. (Pages 203-205)

3) Why did the U.S. War department build Fort St. Michael?
In an effort to dissuade con men that set up gambling tents around St. Michael to make a quick buck off of the prospectors, the U.S. War Department built Fort St. Michael and patrolled the 100-mile perimeter. (Page 207)

4) What were the conditions like on the little steamers coming out of St. Michael? How long was the trip along the Yukon River from St. Michael to Dawson?
Overcrowding on ships heading to the Klondike was the general rule. Small steamers like the SS Amur, designed to carry 160 passengers, were outfitted with temporary quarters and carried as many as 500 passengers. Under optimum conditions, river steamers leaving St. Michael would take more than two weeks to make the 1,700-mile trip. Storms

and other problems hampered navigation along the Yukon and commonly turned the trip into a two-month ordeal. (Pages 206-208)

5) What were the alternate land routes to the Yukon? Why would some prospectors prefer one of the land routes?
Chilkoot Pass and White Pass trails were two alternative land routes. The conditions on the steamers were unreliable, overcrowded and filthy. (Pages 208-209)

DISCUSSION QUESTION

(Discuss this question with your teacher or write your answer in essay form below. Use additional paper if necessary.)

It was a long, hard, expensive journey to get to the Klondike. If you lived during the Klondike Gold Rush period, would you consider making the trip? Why or why not?

_____
_____
_____
_____
_____
_____
_____
_____
_____
_____
_____
_____
_____
_____
_____
_____
_____
_____
_____
_____

TO LEARN MORE

Look for this book at your local library: *Sternwheels on the Yukon,* Arthur Knutson. Snohomish, Washington: Snohomish Publishing Company, 1979

Read more about river transportation in Alaska by visiting http://www.akhistorycourse.org/americas-territory/rivers-get-people-and-freight-inland

MAP ACTIVITY – Locate the following places on the map below using Page 209 of your textbook as a reference:

1) Skagway
2) Deya
3) Chilkoot Trail
4) Sheep Camp
5) The Scales
6) White Pass Trail
7) Bennett
8) Chilkoot Pass

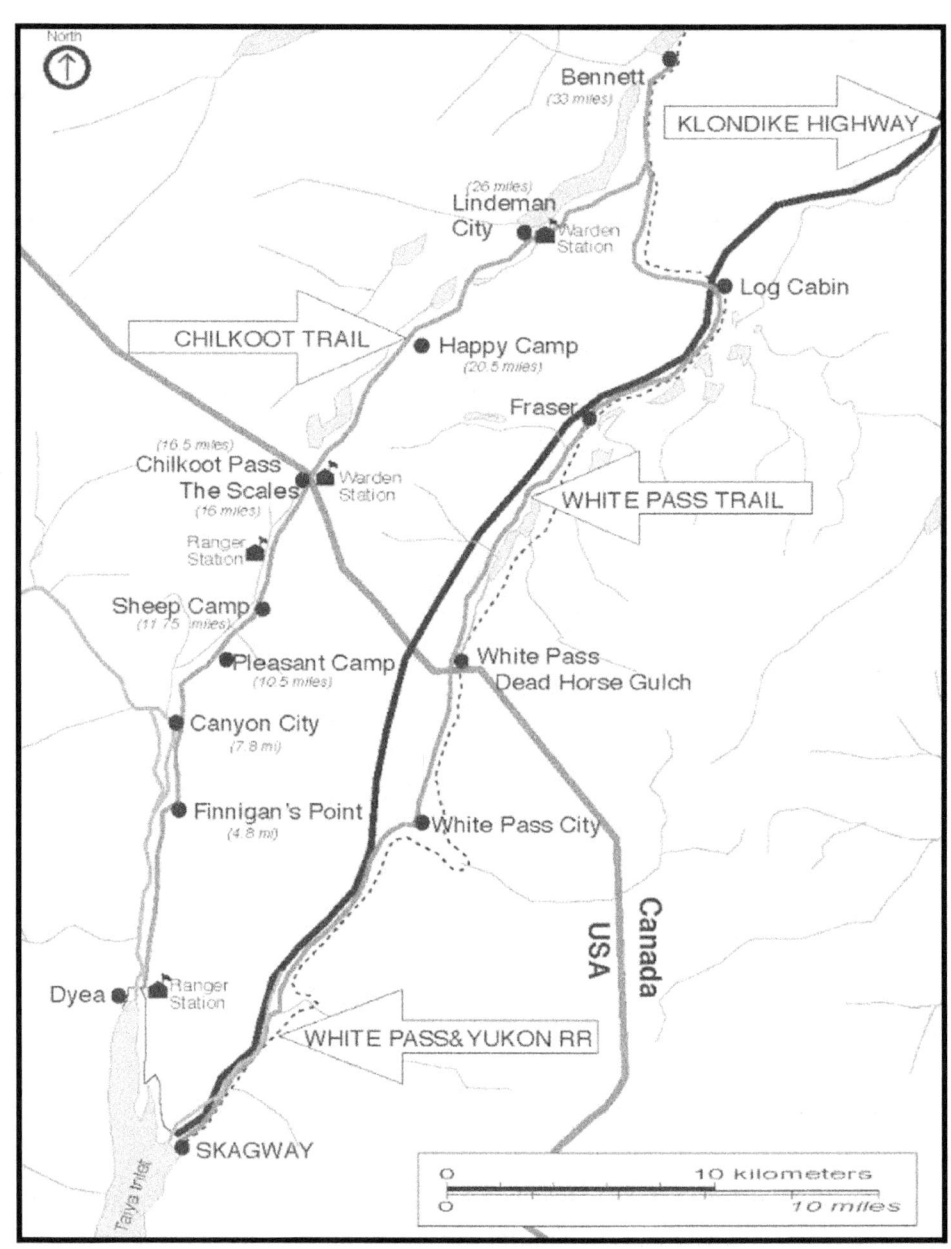

RUSH TO THE KLONDIKE
WORD SEARCH PUZZLE KEY
Find the words in the list below

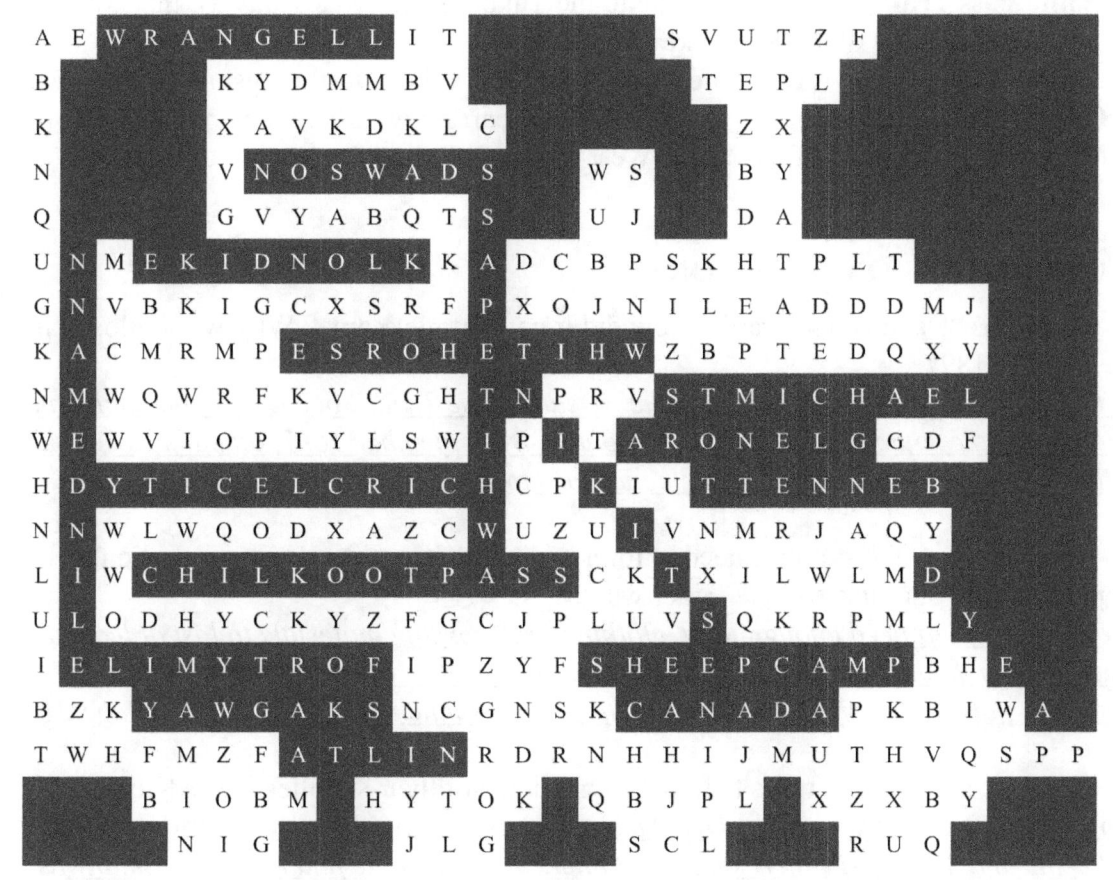

DAWSON	KLONDIKE	CHILKOOT PASS
FORTYMILE	STIKINE	GLENORA
ATLIN	WHITEHORSE	ST MICHAEL
SKAGWAY	DYEA	BENNETT
CIRCLE CITY	WRANGELL	CANADA
SHEEP CAMP	LINDEMANN	WHITE PASS

UNIT 6: RUSH TO THE KLONDIKE

LESSON 24: TRAILS TO GOLD

FACTS TO KNOW:

White Pass Trail – A land trail route to the Yukon, starting at Skagway, that was used at the beginning of the Klondike Gold Rush

Chilkoot Pass Trail – A 33-mile steep trail to the Yukon starting just north of Skagway

Outfit – The load of supplies that a stampeder carried with them on a prospecting trip

Mounties – Members of the North-West Mounted Police, forerunner of Royal Canadian Mounted Police

COMPREHENSION QUESTIONS

1) What was "Dead Horse Trail"? How did it get that nickname? Why was it closed in September 1897?
White Pass eventually earned the name "Dead Horse Trail," because 3,000 pack animals died along the route in less than three months. By September 1897, officials closed the White Pass trail due to the horrible conditions and rotting horse flesh. (Page 211)

2) Name some of the supplies needed for a trip to the Klondike. How much did the typical load of supplies for one miner weigh?
Each man would need enough food, clothing and working materials to last at least one year. Bacon, flour, rice, matches, a gold pan, a tea pot, a whipsaw and whiskey were typically part of an outfit. One outfit could weigh as much as 2,000 pounds. (Page 212)

3) What are some of the ways that the stampeders got their supplies to the Klondike?
Once they reached Skayway or Dyea, many stampeders paid Native packers between 12 cents and $1 to carry their supplies. Others less fortunate had to make as many as 30 trips to shuttle their supplies across the pass, since most couldn't carry more than 70 pounds at a time. (Page 213)

4) What did Mike Mahoney carry up the Chilkoot Trail in an attempt to get it to the Klondike and why? Why was he turned away?
Mike Mahoney carried a piano up the Chilkoot Trail so that six female entertainers and their instruments could continue on to Dawson City to make money from their musical talents. A Mountie told Mahoney that no one would be permitted to bring six women across the border. (Pages 214-217)

5) Almost none of the _100,000_ gold seekers who left for the _Klondike_ in the fall of 1897 by way of the _Stikine River_ trail, _Chilkoot Pass_ trail, the _White Pass_ trail or the all-water route made it to _Dawson_ by the winter. Once they reached _Dawson_ in 1898, most stampeders found the cost of living _high_ and the good gold claims already taken.

DISCUSSION QUESTION

(Discuss this question with your teacher or write your answer in essay form below. Use additional paper if necessary.)

Summarize the options that prospectors had to travel from Seattle to the Yukon. What were the options for all-water routes? What were the options for land routes?

_____
_____
_____
_____
_____
_____
_____
_____
_____
_____
_____
_____
_____
_____
_____

ENRICHMENT ACTIVITY

Imagine that you are a stampeder traveling to the Klondike in 1897. Write a letter to a family member about your adventures. Use what you have learned about the various route options that stampeders had to choose from. Which route did you take? How are the conditions? Who did you meet? What did you see?

TO LEARN MORE

To read more about the Klondike Gold Rush, look for this book at your local library: _One Man's Gold Rush: A Klondike Album._ Seattle: University of Washington Press and Vancouver: Douglas and McIntyre, 1967.

UNIT 6: RUSH TO THE KLONDIKE

LESSON 25: GOLD RUSH TRAILS PHOTO ESSAY

Fill in the blanks:

1) Stampeders traveling from Skagway climbed either the _White Pass_ or _Chilkoot Pass_ trails; and those who took steamers all the way to _St. Michael_ transferred to small boats to chug up the _Yukon_ River to _Dawson_ City.

2) Stampeders loaded up pack horses and hauled their _2,000_-pound outfits up the trails. The _White Pass Trail_ appeared a less arduous route over the mountains than the steep _Chilkoot Pass Trail_, but it had a series of narrow climbs on a rocky switchback path. This route became known as "_Dead Horse Trail_," because 3,000 pack animals died along the trail in less than three months.

3) The majority of stampeders heading to the Klondike chose the _Chilkoot Pass_ Trail. After disembarking at the Southeast Alaska town of _Skagway_, they hiked five miles to Dyea, where they then had the 3,739-foot _Chilkoot Pass_ summit to reach.

4) Shortly after the initial rush, enterprising stampeders rigged an aerial _tramway_ to haul prospectors' _supplies_ up to the summit of the _Chilkoot Pass Trail_ for a fee. Most prospectors didn't have any money to spare, however, and hauled their own _outfits_ up the trail or hired _packers_ for between 12 cents and $1 a load.

5) _Several_ trips were necessary to haul supplies up the _Chilkoot Trail_, as a strong man could not carry more than _70 to 80_ pounds on his back at a time. Stampeders carried _outfits_ that were comprised of items such as: _a sled, shovel, axe, tent, blankets, cooking utensils, whipsaw, flour, dried beans, bacon, tea, tea pot and a gold pan (there are many acceptable answers from the reading)_

6) Klondikers had to pass inspection with _the North-West Mounted Police_ who inspected each _outfit_ to make sure that everyone who crossed over into Canada had the required _provisions for a one-year stay_.

7) Prospectors who finally made it to _Dawson_ City – by way of the all-water, the _White Pass Trail_, _Chilkoot Pass Trail_ or _Stikine_ routes – found the settlement blossoming in the wilderness. However, they also found the _cost of living_ high and most of the _good land_ claimed, so many _turned around and went back home._

8) Three lucky prospectors, _George Washington Carmack, Tagish Charley_ and _Skookum Jim_ discovered gold at _Rabbit Creek (Bonanza Creek)_ on _August 17, 1896_. Most prospectors found _no gold at all._ But the prospect of sudden riches was not all that mattered. For many who made the incredible journey, the Klondike represented _adventure._

ENRICHMENT ACTIVITY

Write your own photo essay using one or two pictures from Chapter 25. Create your own story about what happened in the picture. Write at least one paragraph, and include as many details as possible.

TO LEARN MORE

Klondike Letters: The Correspondence of a Gold Seeker in 1898. Anchorage: Alaska Northwest Publishing Company, 1984. Book insert in The Alaska Journal (4) (Autumn 1984).

UNIT 6: RUSH TO THE KLONDIKE

LESSON 26: JACK DALTON BUILDS TOLL ROAD

FACTS TO KNOW:

Jack Dalton – A frontiersman who opened the Dalton Trail toll road
E.J. Glave – Jack Dalton's companion who helped him explore the toll road route
Dalton Trail – A toll road from Pyramid Harbor on the Lynn Canal in Southeastern Alaska to the Yukon
Toll road – A road that travelers must pay to use

COMPREHENSION QUESTIONS

1) Who was the Dalton Trail named after? When did it open?
The Dalton trail, named after the father of James Dalton whose name has been given to the North Slope Haul Road, opened a route in the 1890s from Pyramid Harbor on the Lynn Canal in Southeastern Alaska to the Yukon. (Page 260)

2) What part of the current Alaska road system in Southeast Alaska did part of this toll road eventually become? _Haines Highway._

3) Jack Dalton left his life on the sea and joined the expedition of _Lt. Frederick Schwatka_ in _1886_ to explore Mount _Saint Elias._

4) Describe Jack Dalton. Why was he so well suited to run a toll road?
Jack Dalton was a short, feisty, stocky frontiersman. He was born for adventure, danger and confrontations. Jack Dalton meant business, and people found he was a tough man. Others had tried to make a toll road work, but Dalton was the only one to make it successful. (Pages 260-262)

5 What purpose did the toll road serve during the gold rush?
Jack Dalton and E.J. Glave decided defective transportation was the sole reason for the undeveloped state of the land. It served a very useful purpose in the gold rush days. About 2,000 beef cattle successfully traveled it – a welcome addition to the miner's food supply. (Page 260)

6) Why was it important that Jack Dalton was able to interact with the Native people? Why did the Natives in the area try to discourage Dalton from opening the toll road?
Dalton's ability to deal with the Indians was very helpful, for this was Indian country they

were traversing. Indians had followed game trails in the vicinity and the proud and warlike Chilkats dominated trade. They never allowed the Interior Indians direct contact with white people. The Chilkats wanted to maintain control of the gate to the Interior. (Page 262)

DISCUSSION QUESTION

(Discuss this question with your teacher or write your answer in essay form below. Use additional paper if necessary.)

The growing population in Alaska provided many new economic opportunities to open businesses, found new cities or open a toll road like Jack Dalton. Name three examples of these economic opportunities from Unit 6.

TO LEARN MORE

Read more about the Dalton Trail and other overland routes in Alaska by visiting: http://www.akhistorycourse.org/americas-territory/overland-routes-develop

TIME TO REVIEW

Review Chapters 22-26 of your book before moving on to the Unit Review. See how many questions you can answer without looking at your book.

UNIT 6: RUSH TO THE KLONDIKE

REVIEW LESSONS 22-26

What do you remember about:

Dawson City – *A city on the Yukon that became the center of the Klondike Gold Rush*

Joseph Ladue – *Founder of Dawson City*

Kate Ryan – *Canadian nurse who traveled to Dawson City for adventure*

St. Michael – *Once a sleepy old Russian village, it became a hub for those coming from and going to the Yukon*

Passenger Steamer – *A little boat typically designed to transport a small number of people, but they were often overcrowded to carry stampeders to and from St. Michael*

All-water route – *Route people took to the Klondike gold fields by steamship from Seattle to St. Michael and then on smaller boats on the Yukon River to Dawson*

White Pass Trail – *A land trail route to the Yukon, starting at Skagway, that was used at the beginning of the Klondike Gold Rush but abandoned soon after because too many animals died on that trail*

Chilkoot Pass Trail – *A 33-mile steep trail to the Yukon starting just north of Skagway*

Outfit – *The load of supplies that a stampeder carried with them on a prospecting trip*

Mounties – *Members of the North-West Mounted Police, forerunner of Royal Canadian Mounted Police*

Jack Dalton – *A frontiersman who opened the Dalton Trail toll road*

E.J. Glave – *Jack Dalton's companion who helped him explore the toll road route*

Dalton Trail – *A toll road from Pyramid Harbor on the Lynn Canal in Southeastern Alaska to the Yukon*

Toll road – *A road that travelers must pay to use*

Fill in the blanks:

1) On *August 28, 1896*, *Joseph Ladue* founded *Dawson* City, named after *George Dawson*, head of the Geological Survey of Canada, who had surveyed the area and noted its possibilities for *gold* a decade before.

2) It's estimated that *100,000* people set out on the rugged journey north, and that between *30,000* and *50,000* actually reached the Klondike area.

3) Dawson became the *largest city* north of San Francisco and west of Winnipeg and boasted nearly 40,000 residents at its height, providing those citizens with *steam heating, running water, electricity and phone service.*

4) In no time at all, Dawson resembled a large cosmopolitan city with *dozens of hotels, motion picture theaters, a hospital and many restaurants.*

5) On June 25, 1897, the sleepy old Russian town of *St. Michael* awoke when the river steamer named *Alice* arrived with 25 miners from *Dawson* carrying $500,000 among them in gold dust.

6) Many of the stampeders heading to the Klondike decided to travel by an all-*water* route. They took large steamships from Seattle to *St. Michael,* but then had to find alternative means to travel the *Yukon* River to *Dawson*. All passengers and cargo had to land at *St. Michael* and transfer to small steamers.

7) Many adventures who chose not to travel the water route through *St. Michael* tackled their choice of two other *land* routes instead: the *White* Pass and the *Chilkoot* Pass trails.

8) The *White* Pass was a less arduous trail over the mountains than the steep *Chilkoot Pass Trail*. It started at Skagway, and the first several miles of *the White* Pass had good road with a gentle upward grade wide enough for *pack animals.* However, it eventually earned the name "*Dead Horse Trail*," because 3,000 *pack animals* died along the route in less than three months.

9) The 33-mile *Chilkoot Pass Trail*, which started one mile from *Dyea*, just north of *Skagway,* also had steep, forbidding grades, but it turned out to be the most direct route to lakes *Lindemann* and *Bennett,* the headwaters of the *Yukon River.*

10) Each man would need enough food, clothing and working materials to last at least *one year.* Other essentials for a gold-seeker's outfit included: *a sled, shovel, axe, tent, blankets, cooking utensils, whipsaw, flour, dried beans, bacon, tea, tea pot and a gold pan (there are many acceptable answers from the reading)*

11) *Jack Dalton*, a feisty man who arrived in Alaska in the 1880s, became a member of *Lt. Frederick Schwatka's* exploration party and established a *toll road* to the Yukon gold fields based on his travels.

12) Parts of that Southeast Alaska toll road can be traveled today along the *Haines Highway.*

Rush to the Klondike
Word Scramble Key
Please unscramble the words below

1.	foCfee	Coffee	A drink made from roasted and ground beanlike seeds, usually served hot
2.	aoBnc	Bacon	Thin strips of cured meat from the sides and belly of a pig
3.	ruoFl	Flour	A powder obtained by grinding grain, typically wheat, and used to make bread
4.	Rcei	Rice	Small white or brown grains that come from Asian plant and used for food
5.	seaBn	Beans	An edible seed, typically kidney-shaped, growing in long pods on certain leguminous plants
6.	hacMets	Matches	A short slender piece of material tipped with a mixture that produces fire when scratched
7.	lsiUsent	Utensils	Forks, spoons and knives, for instance
8.	hltoCnig	Clothing	Things that people wear
9.	Blenatk	Blanket	A covering used especially on a bed to keep you warm
10.	Seohvl	Shovel	A tool with a broad flat blade used for moving dirt

UNIT 6: RUSH TO THE KLONDIKE

UNIT TEST

Choose *three* of the following questions to answer in paragraph form. Use as much detail as possible to completely answer the question.

1) When was Dawson City founded and by whom? Describe how the gold rush impacted Dawson's growth? What luxuries did the city offer?

2) How did St. Michael become a hub for Klondikers? What industries were important in St. Michael because of the gold rush?

3) Describe the all-water routes to the Klondike. Give details of each step that the prospectors needed to take to get to the Klondike. How long did this trip usually take? What were the conditions like?

4) Describe the two major land routes to the Klondike. Give details of each step that the prospectors needed to take to get to the Klondike. What were the conditions like?

5) What was the typical outfit like of a stampeder traveling to the Klondike? How much did it weigh? What was usually included in the outfit?

TEACHER NOTES ABOUT THIS UNIT

Rush to the Klondike
Crossword Puzzle

Read Across and Down clues and fill in blank boxes that match numbers on the clues

Across
1. The top of the Chilkoot Trail is one of these
2. A crude railroad of wooden rails or of wooden rails capped with metal treads
4. Most miners had this – a short coat or jacket made of a thick, heavy woolen cloth, typically with a plaid design
5. The man who founded Dawson
10. Mike Mahoney carried this up the Chilkoot Pass Trail for a troupe of female entertainers
12. Canadian policemen
14. A business that cuts logs into lumber
15. Sleeping quarters on a ship
16. An acquired or natural skill at performing a task
18. Those who were among the first to explore or settle Alaska
20. The buildup of this flammable oily substance caused many fires in gold-rush towns
22. Clothes made from deer hide
24. This man established the only successful toll road into the Klondike area
26. The long tube that takes smoke and gases from a stove up through a roof
30. Woman who came north and became first female constable for North West Mounted Police
31. The title of newspaper stories that is printed in large letters at the top
32. Fire engines that were used from 1860 to 1920
33. Providing an easy and quick way to solve a problem or do something
34. A town like Dawson that grows rapidly as a result of sudden prosperity
35. These pack animals used to carry supplies along gold rush trails

Down
1. A sudden rush of people to the Klondike
3. Involving or requiring strenuous effort; difficult and tiring
6. A high, soft boot worn in the Arctic that is traditionally made from sealskin
7. The *SS Portland* and *SS Excelsior* are both this type of boat
8. More than 1,000 of these were carved into the Chilkoot Pass
9. The men who were paid to carry supplies up the Chilkoot Trail
11. A member of an Indian people of southeastern Alaska belonging to Tlingit group of Indians
13. A person or animal with whom one spends a lot of time or with whom one travels
17. A type of entertainment including short acts, such as comedy, singing and dancing
19. A person, especially a man, who lives in sparsely settled regions
21. A road, trail or section of railroad tracks that has many sharp turns for climbing a steep hill
23. The area at the base of the Chilkoot Trail was called this name
25. A person who searches for gold

Rush to the Klondike
Crossword Puzzle Key

Down (Continued)
27 A natural environment on earth where human activity has not yet reached
28 A large building that offered entertainment to gold rush m1ners
29 A type of handsaw worked by two people
34 A covering of leather, rubber or the like for the foot and lower part of the leg

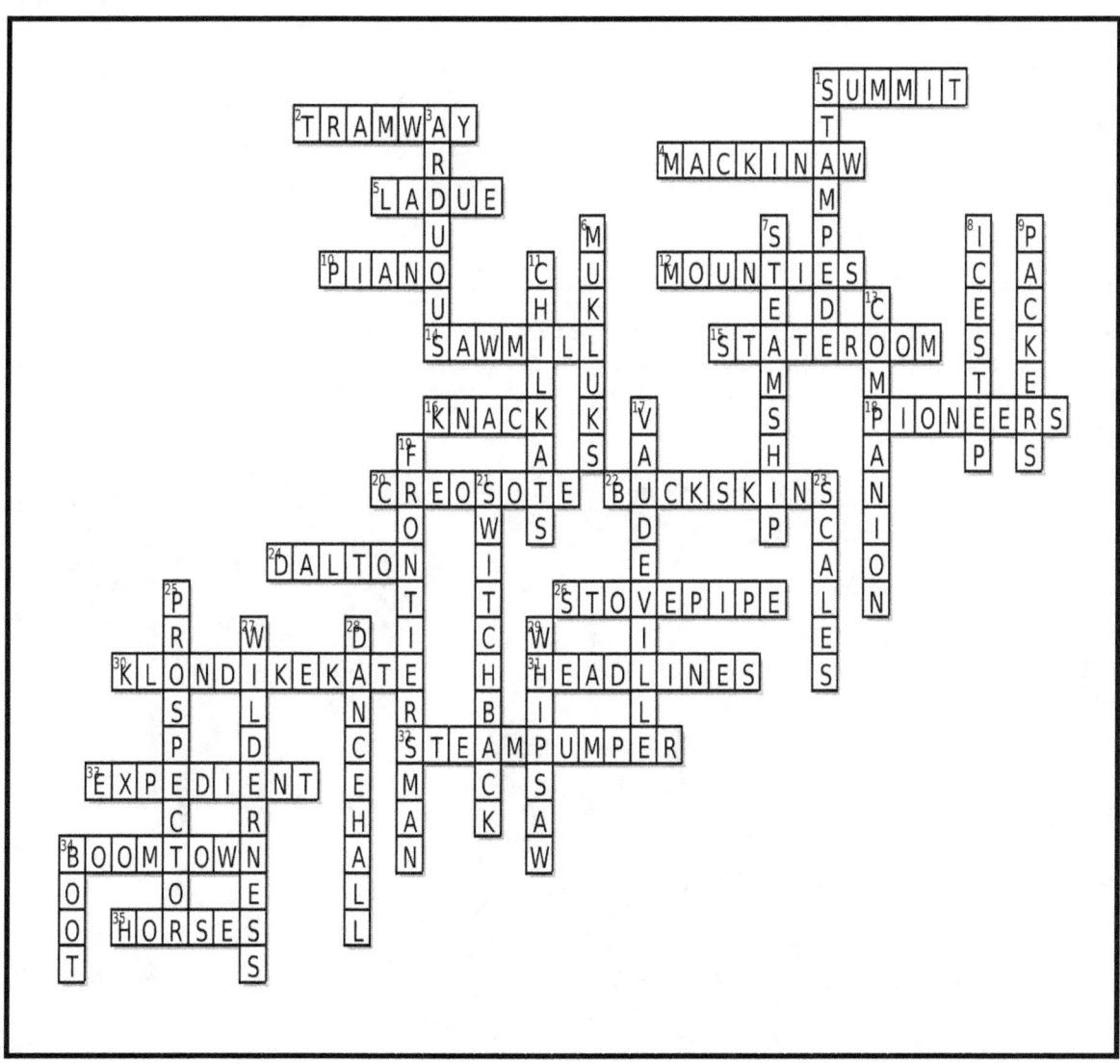

Stampeders could socialize along the Chilkoot Pass Trail, as the photo above taken in 1898 at Sheep Camp shows. The Mascott "hotel" offered hot drinks, meals, lunches and beds. But once the prospectors reached the Klondike gold fields, life could be solitary, as the photo on the bottom shows.

UNIT 7: SEA CAPTAINS, SCOUNDRELS AND NUNS

LESSON 27: SEA CAPTAIN STIFLES MUTINY

FACTS TO KNOW:

Captain Johnny O'Brien – The Irish sea captain of the *Utopia*
Utopia – Captain Johnny O'Brien's steamship
Shanghaied – A term for kidnapping a man and forcing him to work at sea for no pay
Mutiny – Openly refusing to obey someone in authority

COMPREHENSION QUESTIONS

1) What country was Captain Johnny O'Brien from? How did he come to work at sea at the age of 16?
Born in Ireland in 1851, he'd been shanghaied at 16 while traveling home from engineering school in England. (Page 264)

2) Where did the term "shanghaied" come from? How did the California gold rush of 1848 cause a need for more sailors?
The term "shanghaied" can be traced to the mid-1850s, when traders in the Chinese port of Shanghai needed seamen to crew their ships. These unscrupulous merchants would hire thugs to kidnap men who were carousing the bars. Many sailors deserted their ships to seek gold, which left the ships short staffed. (Pages 264-265)

3) What happened when Captain Johnny O'Brien became very ill on the *Utopia*?
O'Brien suffered an attack of acute appendicitis and fell ill. A man on the ship claimed to be a doctor and offered to operate. Volunteers cleared out the galley home of Della Murray Banks, a Denver newspaperwoman who lived on the Homer Spit, for the operation. The former doctor dosed the Captain with whiskey and performed the operation with a kitchen knife and scissors. (Page 266)

4) Who nursed the captain back to health?
Jefferson Randolph Smith, who later became known as "Soapy Smith," the con man who robbed the people of Skagway during the Klondike Gold Rush era.

5) Describe the mutiny that almost occurred on the *Utopia*. Who helped Captain O'Brien?
After his operation, Captain O'Brien ordered his crew to head back to Seattle. His crew refused to continue the trip because the cook was bad. O'Brien asked Jefferson Randolph Smith to give him two revolvers and to help him on deck. He held the chief engineer and

his crew at gunpoint and asked them again if they were going to continue the trip. They quickly changed their minds. (Pages 266-267)

DISCUSSION QUESTION

(Discuss this question with your teacher or write your answer in essay form below. Use additional paper if necessary.)

In this lesson, we learned that men were drugged, kidnapped and forced to work on ships for no pay. What do you think about this practice? Can you think of a better way of convincing someone to come and work on a ship?

_____
_____
_____
_____
_____
_____
_____
_____
_____
_____
_____
_____
_____
_____

ENRICHMENT ACTIVITY

Throughout the remainder of this course, you are going to create your own gold rush short story. Every good story has interesting characters. Brainstorm 3-5 characters that you are going to write about in your gold rush story. What are your characters' names? Where are they from? What do they look like? What is each character's personality like? What are some unique characteristics about each character? Feel free to draw a picture of each of your characters. You will work on the setting and plot of your story in future lessons.

TO LEARN MORE

Look for this book at your local library:
Alaska and the Sea: A Survey of Alaska's Maritime History. By Antonson Mohr, Joan Anchorage: Office of History and Archaeology, Alaska Division of Parks, 1979. Summarizes Alaska's maritime history.

UNIT 7: SEA CAPTAINS, SCOUNDRELS AND NUNS

LESSON 28: SOAPY SMITH HEADS TO SKAGWAY

FACTS TO KNOW:

Soapy Smith – Jefferson Randolph Smith, nicknamed "Soapy," was a skilled criminal
Skagway – Southeastern Alaska city located on the northernmost point of the inside passage
Underworld – A term used to describe the world of organized criminals
Frank H. Reid – Skagway citizen known for giving his life to protect the Committee of 101 from Soapy Smith

COMPREHENSION QUESTIONS

1) Why was Soapy Smith drawn to the Klondike?
Soapy Smith and other con men were drawn to the Klondike in order to make money from the prospectors who were striking it rich during the gold rush. (Page 269)

2) How did Soapy get his nickname?
Soapy gained initial infamy in Denver, Colorado, where he made a fortune from a soap scam. He'd wrap a $100 bill around a bar of soap and slap his own label around that bar. He'd then mix his special soap in a box with numerous other bars, all bearing the name of his new product "Sapolion." He'd walk into a local saloon where a silent partner would randomly buy the $100 soap for $5. He would sell a ton of soap, but the other $100 bars rarely surfaced. (Page 269)

3) How did Soapy Smith's telegraph office get gold from miners?
Soapy Smith and his men built a telegraph office. Miners came into the office to telegraph news of their strikes to folks back home. A few hours later, a telegraphed reply came back – usually asking the prospectors to send money. The helpful telegraph employees happily wired the miners' gold dust in return. There was only one problem. The telegraph wires extended only a few feet into Skagway's harbor. (Pages 270-271)

4) Why did a committee of Skagway residents decide to run Soapy out of town?
Soapy ran a saloon-casino that cheated customers out of their money. He ran a telegraph scheme to steal money from prospectors who thought they were sending money home to loved ones. A meeting of citizens was called to discuss the murder of a miner named H. Bean as well as other crimes, which resulted in 101 citizens issuing a warning for all con men to leave Skagway. (Page 271)

5) How did Soapy Smith die? Where is he buried?
Soapy and his gang tried to crash a meeting of the Committee of 101 on July 8, 1898. Frank H. Reid was guarding the entrance of the meeting place. When Soapy attempted to get into the meeting, Reid shot him. Soapy fired his gun back. Soapy died on the spot and Reid died 12 days later. (Page 272)

DISCUSSION QUESTION

(Discuss this question with your teacher or write your answer in essay form below. Use additional paper if necessary.)

The Klondike Gold Rush inspired men and women from all over the world to come to Alaska. Consider all of the people that you have learned about who traveled to the Klondike during the gold rush period. What is your favorite story and why? Was this person seeking gold, adventure, fame or something else?

_____
_____
_____
_____
_____
_____
_____
_____
_____
_____
_____
_____

ENRICHMENT ACTIVITY

Now that you have brainstormed your characters, it is time to think about the setting of your story. Will your story take place on the Yukon River? Dawson City? Skagway? Cape Nome (which you will learn about in the next lesson)? Do you want to write a story that takes place in your fictional city from Lesson 22? Write a short paragraph to describe your setting. What does it look like? What does it smell like? What important landmarks are located there? You will work on the plot of your story during the next lessons.

TO LEARN MORE

Look for this book at your local library:
Southeast: Alaska's Panhandle, Alaska Geographic Society, Vol. 5, No. 2, 1978.

Soapy Smith
Word Search Puzzle Key
Find the words listed below

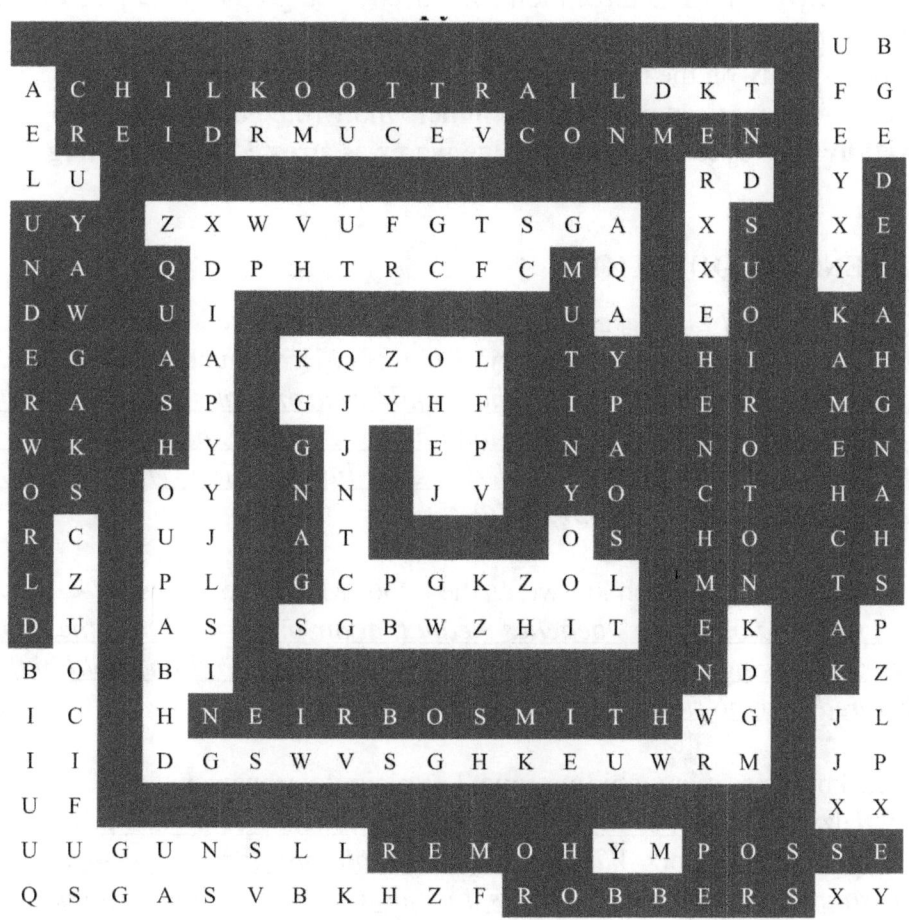

MUTINY	SHANGHAIED	HOMER
QUASH	NOTORIOUS	GANG
HENCHMEN	UNDERWORLD	POSSE
SKAGWAY	CHILKOOT TRAIL	CON MEN
ROBBERS	SOAPY	SMITH
REID	KATCHEMAK	O'BRIEN

UNIT 7: SEA CAPTAINS, SCOUNDRELS AND NUNS

LESSON 29: MINERS STAMPEDE TO NOME

FACTS TO KNOW:

Three Lucky Swedes – The three men who discovered gold near Cape Nome in 1898 that spurred the Poor Man's Gold Rush

Cape Nome – A city on the northern shore of the Norton Sound in Alaska

Rex Beach – An American novelist and miner who wrote gold rush novels

Judge Arthur H. Noyes – A corrupt judge who was arrested for exploiting claimants in Nome

COMPREHENSION QUESTIONS

1) *John Brynteson, Jafet Lindberg* and *Eric Lindblom* discovered gold that started the Nome gold rush. When did they make their discovery? How much gold did they find?
Swedish sailor Eric Lindblom, Jafet Lindberg and Swedish coal miner John Brynteson all ended up in Nome because the promising land in the Klondike already had been claimed. Their Anvil Creek discovery in 1898 yielded $3.5 million in gold by 1900 and 80 million over the next two decades. (Pages 275-276)

2) Why was the Nome gold rush known as the "Poor Man's Gold Rush"?
The discovery of gold on Nome's beaches meant that anyone could work the public property without staking or recording claims. Those who hadn't found gold in the Klondike poured into the Nome area. (Page 276)

3) Was Nome known as a law-abiding town? Explain your answer.
No. The town was filled with shady characters and hardened criminals who didn't pay much attention to mining laws. With more than 60 saloons, dozens of criminals, a few hundred prostitutes and dishonest officials, including an embezzling postmaster, a tax assessor who went to prison for illicit financial dealings and a judge who made crooked dealings, it's not surprising that robberies and murders flourished in Nome. (Page 277)

4) What inspired novelist Rex Beach to write novels about the gold rush? What was the title of one of his famous gold rush novels?
Beach learned about the gold rush during his own prospecting trips. One of his most famous novels, "The Spoilers," tells the tale of the conniving Nome judge, Arthur H. Noyes. (Pages 279-280)

5) How did the Poor Man's Gold Rush end? When?
The Poor Man's Gold Rush played itself out by the end of 1900. After a fierce storm in 1900, and a huge fire destroyed the business district and the beach mining operations in 1905, thousands left on boats heading south. (Page 285)

DISCUSSION QUESTION

(Discuss this question with your teacher or write your answer in essay form below. Use additional paper if necessary.)

Why do you think there was so much crime in Nome? Think back to the different stories that you have read about in this chapter and previous chapters.

_____
_____
_____
_____
_____
_____
_____
_____
_____
_____
_____
_____
_____
_____
_____

ENRICHMENT ACTIVITY

Now that you have brainstormed your characters and setting, it's time to think about the plot of your story. Brainstorm some ideas for your exciting gold rush story. Write down two or three possible story ideas. You will begin writing a rough draft of your story in the next lesson.

TO LEARN MORE

Read more about the Nome Gold Rush by visiting http://www.akhistorycourse.org/north-west-and-arctic/1897-1920-gold

UNIT 7: SEA CAPTAINS, SCOUNDRELS AND NUNS

LESSON 30: SISTERS OF PROVIDENCE HEAD TO NOME

FACTS TO KNOW:

Sisters of Providence – Four nuns who built the first hospital in Nome
Holy Cross Hospital – First hospital that opened in Nome on July 15, 1902
Fairbanks – The largest city in the interior region of Alaska
Anchorage – Alaska's largest city, located in southcentral Alaska

COMPREHENSION QUESTIONS

1) Why did the Sisters of Providence come to Nome? How did they travel to get there?
At the urging of two Jesuit priests, the sisters traveled to Nome to build a much-needed hospital for the more than 20,000 prospectors that were flooding the city. After nine days of seasickness aboard the SS Senator, the sisters' voyage ended with a 72-hour smallpox quarantine. (Page 287)

2) What kind of medical attention did the people of Nome receive before the sisters started their work there?
Before arrival of the Sisters of Providence, the miners relied on home remedies, often set their own broken bones and sometimes used Native healing methods. (Page 287)

3) How did the sisters pay for the hospital?
The nuns regularly visited the mines – on foot, horseback or dog sled – to solicit donations. They also sold tickets, as a form of insurance, for hospital care: $3 bought the miner a one month stay, $12 for six months and $24 for one year. The price included board, medicines, milk and liquor – as ordered by a doctor – as well as the use of bathroom and the operating room. The town also held annual carnivals to help fund the hospital. (Pages 288-290)

4) Why did the Nome mission close in 1918?
The survival of the hospital and school depended upon the financial health of Nome's population, which peaked in 1907-08. By 1918 the mining industry had pretty much disappeared, and the Nome mission was forced to close its doors on Sept. 20 after 16 years of service. (Page 290)

5) What other areas of Alaska did the Sisters of Providence serve?
While busy with Holy Cross Hospital of Nome, they also were busy in the new gold rush town of Fairbanks, founded in 1903. The sisters took over ownership of St. Joseph's Hospital in 1911. In 1938, the sisters decided there was a need for medical care in Anchorage, which was established in 1915. (Pages 291-292)

ENRICHMENT ACTIVITY

Using your brainstorming notes, characters, setting and plot, write a rough draft of your short story. Don't worry about grammar, spelling or punctuation on this draft. You will have time to edit your draft in the next lesson.

TO LEARN MORE

Read more about medicine in early Alaska by visiting http://www.akhistorycourse.org/americas-territory/alaskas-heritage/chapter-4-21-health-and-medicine

Most stampeders that made their way to Nome following the discovery of gold by the Three Lucky Swedes in the late 1890s had tents in the outfits they brought with them. With trees far and few between in the region, some adventurers relied on driftwood to help keep their shelters secure on windy days.

The information with this photograph said the miner shown here on the Nome beach in 1905 is Joseph Shaw, age 73.

MAP ACTIVITY

Identify the following cities on the map:
1) Nome
2) Fairbanks
3) Anchorage

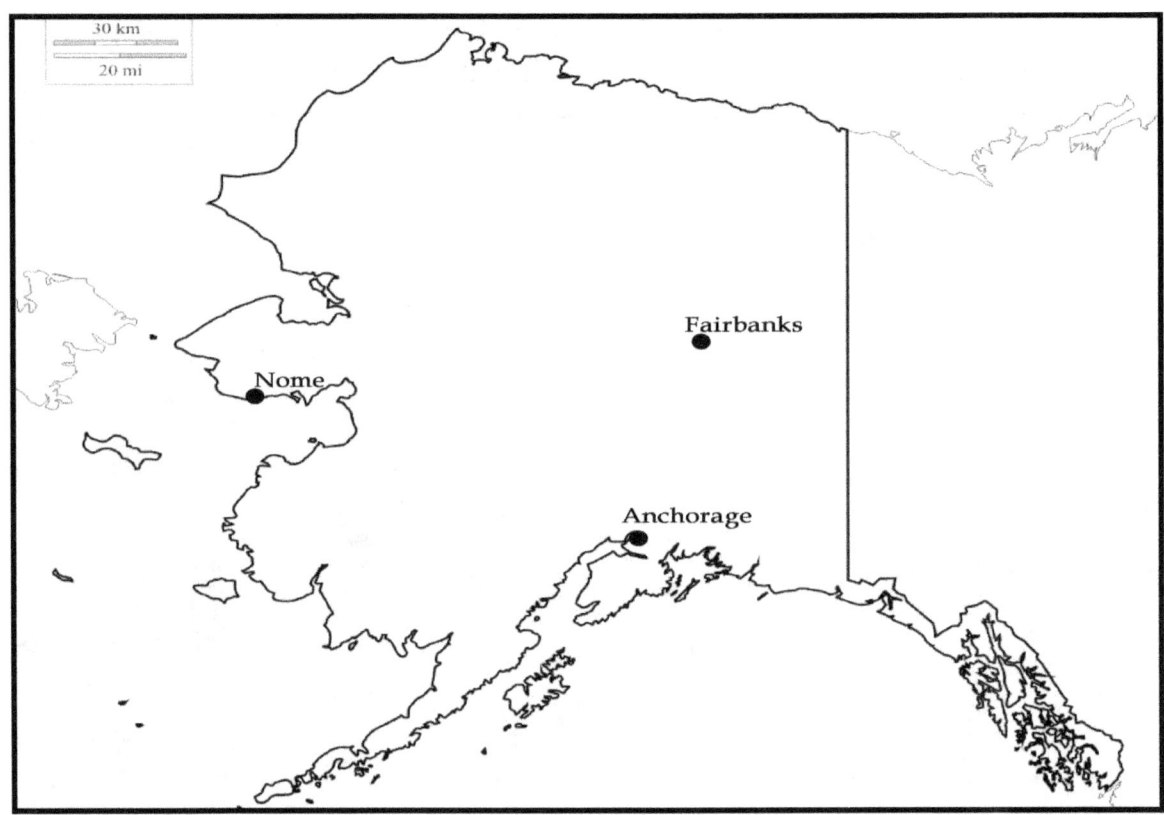

UNIT 8: GOLD RUSH IMPACTS NATIVES

LESSON 31: NATIVES AND THE RUSH FOR GOLD

FACTS TO KNOW:

Chilkats – Tlingit Indians along the Chilkat River and on Chilkat Peninsula
Chilkoots – Tlingit Indians along the Taku River
Southern Tutchone – Indian people of the Athabaskan-speaking group living mainly in the southern Yukon area of Canada

COMPREHENSION QUESTIONS

1) Summarize the editorial in the 1900 Dawson newspaper that voiced concern over the treatment of Alaska's indigenous peoples.
The Native people of Alaska have had their land taken away from them without permission. The game that they depend on for subsistence is disappearing. Native people used to own all of the land and everything in it. Everything has been taken from them. While it may not be against the law, it is morally wrong. (Pages 293-294)

2) How did the influx of white traders, prospectors and settlers change the Native's way of life?
For some, whites brought illness, alcohol, destruction of hunting grounds and forests and disregard of traditional lifestyles. (Page 294)

3) In what ways did Native people help the miners?
Native people trapped, hunted and fished for the miners who trickled into the territory. They also provided transportation for men, messages and supplies, and they saved many lives by helping those who were ill prepared for Alaska's elements. Native people traded fur and other important items that the prospectors needed. (Pages 294-295)

4) How did the Native people profit from the prospectors?
Some Native people profited from the prospectors through trade. They would also carry supplies on their backs or on a boat for a fee. (Pages 295-300)

5) How was the traditional Native way of life changed by missionaries?
The well-intentioned missionaries discouraged Natives from drinking, gambling and carousing with the non-Native miners. Many missionaries discouraged Natives from speaking their languages and changed their methods of worship. (Page 300)

DISCUSSION QUESTION

(Discuss this question with your teacher or write your answer in essay form below. Use additional paper if necessary.)

How did many non-Natives view the indigenous people of Alaska?

_____
_____
_____
_____
_____
_____
_____
_____
_____
_____
_____
_____
_____
_____
_____
_____
_____

ENRICHMENT ACTIVITIY

It's time to write the final draft of your gold rush short story. Read over your rough draft and correct any mistakes you made. Rewrite your corrected final draft. Share your final story with the class.

TO LEARN MORE

Look for this book at your local library:
Tlingit Stories, Maria Ackerman. Anchorage: Alaska Methodist University Press, 1975. A collection of legends from Southeast Alaska.

Tlingit Country Southeast

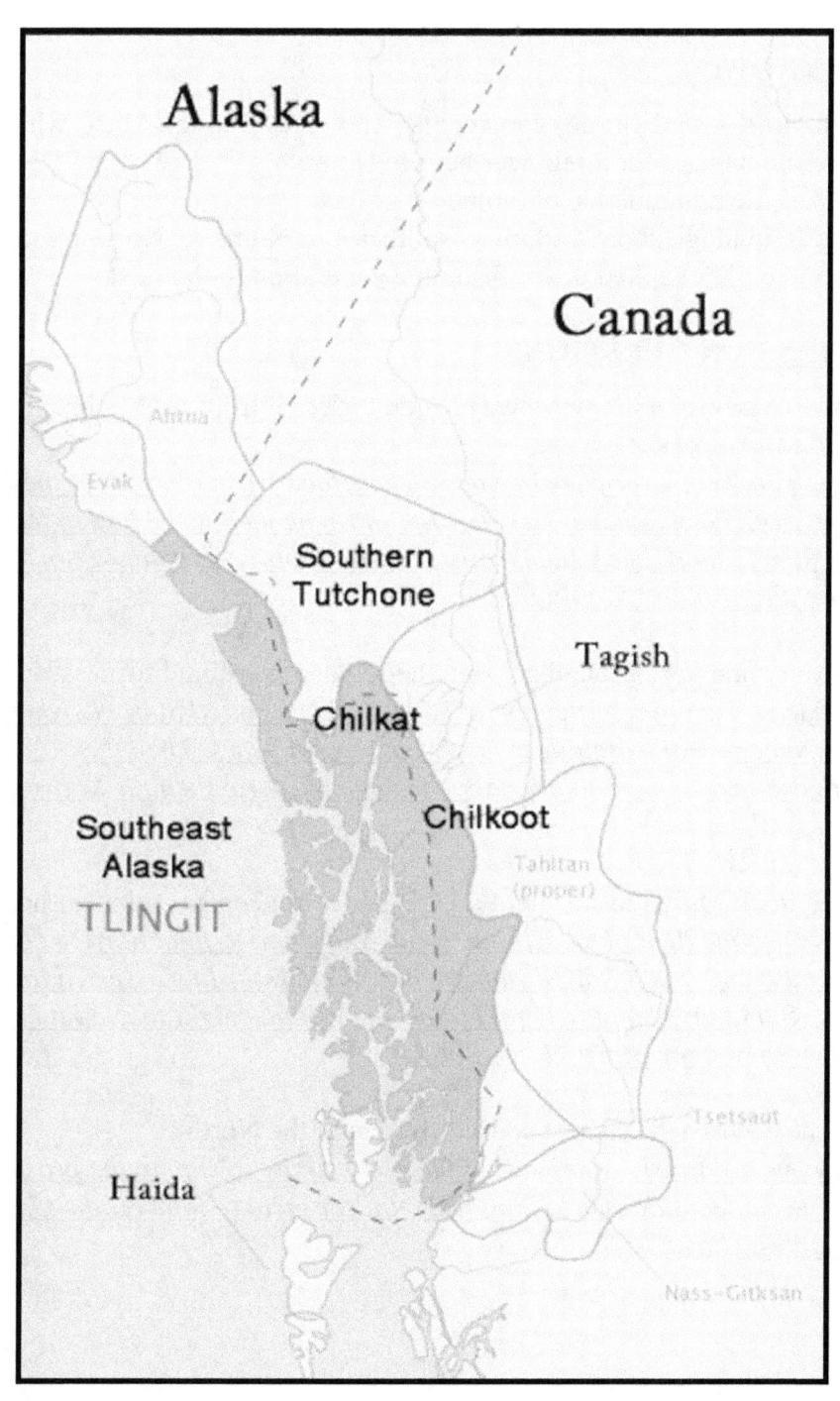

UNIT 8: GOLD RUSH IMPACTS NATIVES

LESSON 32: RICHEST NATIVE WOMAN IN THE NORTH

FACTS TO KNOW:

Mary Makrikoff – An Eskimo woman, also known as Sinrock Mary, who helped the U.S. government care for a reindeer herd in Nome
Sinrock – A settlement outside of Nome
Unalakleet – A village about 148 miles southeast of Nome on Norton Sound
Legacy – Something handed down from one generation to the next

COMPREHENSION QUESTIONS

1) According to Mary, in what ways was Nome different from St. Michael? What languages did Mary speak?
There were no people or groceries in Nome. Their food wasn't like what the Eskimos of St. Michael worked hard to have. Her new life in Nome meant she had to learn how to live on "real simple food, like whale meat, seal oil, rabbits and ptarmigan." Mary spoke fluent Inupiaq, English and Russian. (Page 304)

2) How did Mary and her husband get into the reindeer herding business?
Mary and Charlie lived in a settlement outside of Nome called Sinrock, where they helped the U.S. government with its reindeer herds for several years. Then the government gave the couple 500 animals, thus making them the first Natives to be given their own herd. (Page 306)

3) Why did Sinrock Mary have to fight a legal battle to keep her reindeer herd?
When Mary's husband died of measles in 1900, Mary had to fight hard to keep her reindeer. Because she was a Native woman, her brothers-in-law asserted that she couldn't own property. But after a lengthy legal battle, she won the right to keep half the herd and became known as Sinrock Mary. (Page 306)

4) How did she become the richest Native woman in the North?
During the Nome gold rush, Mary seized the opportunity to supply the prospectors with fresh meat. She made a tidy sum selling her reindeer meat to miners, the U.S. Army station and stores. (Page 307)

5) Why did Mary leave Nome in 1901?
Mary constantly had to dodge gold-rush prospectors who wanted her reindeer for food, as well as to haul supplies and equipment to their claims. When she refused to give them the animals, the men called her names and shot at the reindeer to scatter the herd. She got fed up with the constant pestering in 1901 and moved to Unalakleet. (Pages 307-308)

DISCUSSION QUESTION

(Discuss this question with your teacher or write your answer in essay form below. Use additional paper if necessary.)

What was Reindeer Mary's legacy?

_____
_____
_____
_____
_____
_____
_____
_____
_____
_____
_____
_____
_____
_____
_____
_____
_____

TO LEARN MORE

Look for this book at your local library:
The Eskimos and Aleuts. By Dumond, Don E., London: Thames and Hudson, 1979.

TIME TO REVIEW

Review Chapters 27-32 of your book before moving on to the Unit Review. See how many questions you can answer without looking at your book.

UNIT 7: SEA CAPTAINS, SCOUNDRELS AND NUNS
UNIT 8: GOLD RUSH IMPACTS NATIVES

REVIEW LESSONS 27-32

What do you remember about:

Captain Johnny O'Brien – <u>The Irish Sea Captain of the Utopia</u>

Utopia – <u>Captain Johnny O'Brien's steamship</u>

Shanghaied – <u>A term for kidnapping a man and forcing him to work at sea with no pay</u>

Mutiny – <u>Openly refusing to obey someone in authority</u>

Soapy Smith – <u>His given name was Jefferson Randolph Smith, and he was a skilled criminal</u>

Skagway – <u>Southeast Alaska city located on the northernmost point of the inside passage</u>

Underworld – <u>A term used to describe the world of organized criminals</u>

Frank H. Reid – <u>Skagway citizen known for giving his life to protect the Committee of 101 from Soapy Smith</u>

Three Lucky Swedes – <u>The three men who discovered gold near Cape Nome in 1898 that spurred the Poor Man's Gold Rush</u>

Cape Nome – <u>A city on the northern shore of the Norton Sound in Alaska</u>

Rex Beach – <u>An American novelist and miner who wrote gold rush novels</u>

Judge Arthur H. Noyes – <u>A corrupt judge who was arrested for exploiting claimants in Nome</u>

Sisters of Providence – <u>Four nuns who built the first hospital in Nome</u>

Holy Cross Hospital – <u>First hospital that opened in Nome on July 15, 1902</u>

Fairbanks – *The largest city in the interior region of Alaska*

Anchorage – *The largest city in Alaska, located in southcentral Alaska*

Chilkats – *Tlingit Indians along the Chilkat River and on Chilkat Peninsula*

Chilkoots – *Tlingit Indians along the Taku River*

Southern Tutchone – *Indian people of the Athabaskan-speaking group living mainly in the southern Yukon area of Canada*

Mary Makrikoff – *An Eskimo woman, also known as Sinrock Mary, who helped the U.S. government care for a reindeer herd in Nome*

Sinrock – *A settlement outside of Nome*

Unalakleet – *A village about 148 miles southeast of Nome on Norton Sound*

Legacy – *Something handed down from one generation to the next*

Fill in the blanks:

1) At age 16, *Captain Johnny O'Brien* was *shanghaied* into working on a ship for six years. When he finally worked his way back to his home country of *Ireland*, he found out his parents had died.

2) A man traveling to Cook Inlet volunteered to nurse *Utopia* Captain *Johnny O'Brien* back to health following an operation to remove his *appendix*. That mystery man turned out to be none other than *Jefferson Randolph Smith*, better known to Alaskans as "Soapy."

3) The *Soapy Smith* Gang terrorized the people of *Skagway* during the late 1890s. A committee of residents finally organized a group to run *Soapy Smith* and his gang out of town.

4) The *Committee of 101* called a meeting on the dock on July 8, 1898, and placed *Frank H. Reid* to guard the entrance.

5) Both *Soapy Smith* and *Frank H. Reid* died from gunshot wounds as a result of a confrontation at the meeting of *the Committee of 101*.

6) America's last big placer gold rush came in *1898*, when gold was discovered at *Anvil Creek* by three greenhorn Scandinavians.

7) Known as the *"Poor Man's Gold Rush,"* the discovery of gold on *Nome*'s beaches shortly after the Anvil Creek discovery meant that anyone could work the public property without staking or recording claims.

8) The influx of more than *20,000* prospectors working the gold-filled beaches of *Nome* brought with it the desperate need for *medical* facilities. Before the arrival of the *Sisters of Providence*, the miners relied upon *home remedies*, often set their own broken bones and sometimes used *Native healing* methods.

9) The *Sisters of Providence* opened the doors to *Holy Cross* hospital July 15, 1902.

10) At the time of the *U.S.* purchase of Alaska, most *Alaska Natives* lived the traditional lifestyles of their ancestors, *hunting and fishing* for a living and governing themselves through ancient tribal systems. For some, the whites brought *illness, alcohol, destruction of hunting grounds and forests and disregard of traditional lifestyles*.

11) Born to an Inupiat Eskimo mother and a Russian trader father, *Mary Makrikoff* was raised in *St. Michael*. Her successful *reindeer herding* business made her the *richest* Native woman in the North.

12) When *Reindeer Mary* died in 1948, she left a *legacy* of compassion and generosity. People still tell stories about how she shared her wealth the *Eskimo* way.

Alaska Natives and the Rush for Gold
Word Scramble Key
Please unscramble the words below

1.	ednonisigu	indigenous	First people to live in a place
2.	neatnci	ancient	Very old, belonging to the very distant past
3.	irtbe	tribe	A group of people that includes many families and relatives who have the same language, customs and beliefs
4.	osiuetanc	tenacious	Not easily letting go or giving up
5.	neiws	sinew	A piece of tough fibrous tissue uniting muscle to bone, or bone to bone, that Natives used in sewing animal skin
6.	ahlenouc	eulachon	Small oil-rich fish
7.	enrderei	reindeer	Domesticated caribou used for food during Nome gold rush
8.	qnpaiiu	inupiaq	Inupiat Eskimo language
9.	roisnkc	sinrock	Settlement outside of Nome
10.	aaekunllte	unalakleet	Village where Reindeer Mary moved after winning the right to keep her reindeer herd

UNIT 7: SEA CAPTAINS, SCOUNDRELS AND NUNS
UNIT 8: GOLD RUSH IMPACTS NATIVES

UNIT TEST

Choose *three* of the following questions to answer in paragraph form. Use as much detail as possible to completely answer the question.

1) Who was Captain Johnny O'Brien? How did he begin working on a ship at age 16? What happened when he became ill aboard his ship?

2) Describe Jefferson Randolph Smith. How did the people of Skagway stop him from terrorizing their city?

3) Why was the Nome Gold Rush called the "Poor Man's Gold Rush"?

4) Who were the Sisters of Providence? What did they do to serve the people of Nome?

5) In what ways did the influx of white prospectors, settlers and traders change the Native way of life in Alaska?

6) Who was the richest Native woman of the North? How did she make her riches? What legacy did she leave?

_____
_____
_____
_____
_____
_____
_____
_____
_____
_____
_____
_____
_____
_____
_____
_____
_____
_____

TEACHER NOTES ABOUT THIS UNIT

TEACHER NOTES

TEACHER NOTES

TEACHER NOTES

www.ingramcontent.com/pod-product-compliance
Lightning Source LLC
Chambersburg PA
CBHW082125230426
43671CB00015B/2807